The Complete

IDIOT'S

Pocket Reference to

DOS 6.2

Jennifer Fulton

**alpha
books**

A Division of Macmillan Computer Publishing

201 West 103rd Street, Indianapolis, Indiana 46290 USA

For my mother-in-law Maria, who manages to have fun with her computer, despite the fact that it uses DOS.

International Standard Book Number: 1-56761-516-3

Library of Congress Catalog Card Number:

96 95 94   8 7 6 5 4 3 2 1

Interpretation of the printing code: the rightmost number of the second series of numbers is the number of the book's printing. For example, a printing code of 94-1 shows that the first printing of the book occurred in 1994.

Printed in the United States of America

Screen reproductions in this book were created by means of the program Collage Plus from Inner Media, Inc., Hollis, NH.

Publisher

   Marie Butler-Knight

Managing Editor

   Elizabeth Keaffaber

Product Development Manager

   Faithe Wempen

Acquisitions Manager

   Barry Pruett

Production Editor

   Phil Kitchel

Manuscript Editor

   Barry Childs-Helton

Book Designer

   Barbara Webster

Index

   Chris Cleveland

Production

   Gary Adair, Dan Caparo, Brad Chinn, Kim Cofer,
   Jennifer Eberhardt, Erika Millen, Beth Rago, Bobbi
   Satterfield, Karen Walsh, Robert Wolf

**Special Thanks to C. Herbert Feltner for ensuring the
technical accuracy of this book.**

Contents

Introduction

You are an intelligent, mature adult. You know how to balance a budget, book a one-day meeting in Chicago at the last minute, and get the copier to collate (and staple!). Yet when it comes to DOS, you sometimes feel like an idiot.

Well, you're not alone.

DOS is a complex, archaic old lady held over from the days when computers occupied entire rooms, much less desktops. But the old gal is still around, so you're stuck dealing with her. And she's a very temperamental old thing, so when you talk to her, you better do it in a quiet voice or she'll whack your hands with her cane. (Temperamental people tend to do things like that.)

So Why Can't I Live Without This Book?

With so many computer books on the market, why do you need this one? Well, first off, this book doesn't assume that you know anything at all about how to use DOS (or that you want to start learning).

In addition, instead of cryptic I-know-what-to-type-but-I'm-not-going-to-tell-you command listings, such as:

```
MEM [/classify ¦ /debug ¦ /free ¦ /
module programname] [/page]
```

This DOS reference fully explains every term, every instruction—and *in English!* (Imagine that!)

Short, clear, step-by-step instructions tell you exactly what to type, so you can't make a mistake. In addition, the light-hearted tone makes it easier to deal with DOS when you'd rather be having your nails pulled out one by one. Simply open the book when you have a question or problem, read what you need to, and get back to your life.

This book is designed for the person who:

➤ Likes alphabetized lists.

➤ Doesn't want to poke around in a large manual.

➤ Wants just the necessary steps to accomplish a specific task, minus all the technical mumbo-jumbo.

➤ Wants to put something in their last empty pocket.

What Do I Need to Know to Use This Book?

First, this book is divided into several sections so you can find what you need quickly:

➤ **The Least You Need to Know About DOS**   A quickie guide to entering DOS commands without fear.

➤ **Bossing DOS: A DOS Command Reference**   Alphabetized reference to the most commonly used DOS commands, with step-by-step instructions on how to use them correctly.

➤ **Hacking Away at Files With the DOS Editor**   Guide to using the DOS Editor with the least amount of fuss.

➤ **More Than You'll Want to Know About Config-uring Your PC**   The mysteries of AUTOEXEC.BAT and CONFIG.SYS revealed!

➤ **Playing the DOS Shell Game**   How to use the DOS Shell to avoid that nasty prompt forever.

➤ **Help! It's an Error Message!**   When DOS gives you an error message in Babylonian, this section helps you decipher it into English and to decide what to do.

Just thumb to the section you need, and you'll find step-by-step instructions to get you out of whatever trouble DOS got you into. Each section is self-contained, with exactly what you need to know to solve your problem or to answer your question.

If you need outside help, never fear. For inside this pocket reference, you'll find several references to the Big Daddy version of this book, *The Complete Idiot's Guide to DOS, New Edition*, where you'll be treated to a cup of coffee and more gossip about your old friends, the DOS commands. If you don't own a copy of Big Daddy, you can still get one wherever bright orange books are sold.

This book also gives you visual clues (some in Alpha Books 3-D) so you'll know exactly what to do:

> When you need to type something, it appears like this: **TYPE THIS COMMAND**.

> If you need to type something, but you have to substitute your own information (such as the name of a file), it appears like this: *filename.ext*.

> If you're supposed to press a particular key (such as the Spacebar), that key appears like this:
> [Spacebar].

> The Enter key appears like this: [↵Enter].

> Just so you won't explode with happiness while working with DOS, some steps are optional. So skip the steps marked **(Optional)** if you want.

> If you're working in one of the *graphical* (i.e., pretty) DOS utilities such as MSBACKUP, you'll be told what to click on with your mouse (no archaic keyboard instructions here). For example, if you need to click on the File menu to open it, it appears like this: **File**.

Finally, there are some special notes that I've used in this book to help you along the way:

Notes and tips showing the easiest way to perform some task.

Special hints and amusing examples on how to use this particular DOS command.

Acknowledgments

Actually, how this book came to be is a complete mystery to me. But here's a list of those who helped:

> Thanks to Faithe Wempen for your insight and guidance.

> Thanks to Kelly Oliver for her hard work on the sample for this series. It really got me up and writing fast!

> Thanks to Barry Childs-Helton and Phil Kitchel for their marvelous editing job.

> Thanks to all of you who've waded through too many DOS manuals which never explained what to do, that you made this book a necessity.

Trademarks

All terms mentioned in this book that are known to be trademarks or service marks are listed below. In addition, terms suspected of being trademarks or service marks have been appropriately capitalized. Alpha Books cannot attest to the accuracy of this information. Use of a term in this book should not be regarded as affecting the validity of any trademark or service mark.

The Least You Need to Know About DOS

OK, so you bought this book. Good start. Maybe you're ready to dive right in and try out a command. In that case, this section may not be for you, because it's for those of us who dip our toes in *before* we take a dive into murky waters (and believe me, you can't get any murkier than DOS). In this section, you'll learn enough about DOS to get your feet wet, but not enough to feel you got soaked.

What's a DOS Prompt?

The *DOS prompt* is a message from DOS telling you that it's waiting for a command. Think of the prompt as a college intern who follows you around, begging you to give him something to do.

When you type a command, it appears next to the prompt on-screen. Typical DOS prompts include **C>** or **C:\DOS>**. Next to the prompt you'll find the *cursor*—a horizontal blinking line that follows what you type the way a car salesman follows you around the lot when he senses you have lots of cash and believe him when he says this car has never been in an accident and might buy anything just to get rid of him. When you type com-mands, they appear on-screen wherever the cursor is located.

Customize your DOS prompt so that it changes as you move between different drives and directories.

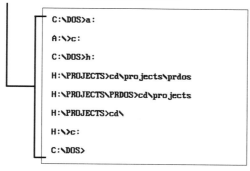

```
C:\DOS>a:

A:\>c:

C:\DOS>h:

H:\PROJECTS>cd\projects\prdos

H:\PROJECTS\PRDOS>cd\projects

H:\PROJECTS>cd\

H:\>c:

C:\DOS>
```

What's Your DOS Version?

Some commands are only included with the latest DOS versions—DOS 6, 6.2, DOS 6.21, and DOS 6.22. (By the way, DOS *versions* are numbered consecutively; DOS 4 was followed by DOS 5, which was followed by DOS 6, etc.) To see what DOS version you have:

1. Type **VER**.

2. Press ⏎Enter.

As long as you see something like DOS version 6.2 or 6.21, or 6.22, you're fine. If you don't, you may not be able to use all of the commands listed in this book.

Don't reach for that receipt so fast: you can probably still learn a lot from this book even if you don't have DOS 6.x, because most of the commands in earlier versions are still a part of DOS.

Things You Should Know Before You Use DOS

We all do it. While a stewardess is busy explaining complex safety procedures which might just save our undeserving souls when or if the plane decides to take a siesta, we're popping peanuts and browsing through the latest issue of "In-Flight Shopper." Let's face it—some things you just don't want to know unless you absolutely have to. Here's a list of the absolutely-have-to-knows for DOS, which you should learn about now, before you do something silly and your computer goes down in fiery ruin. Okay, so your computer *won't* catch on fire, no matter what buttons you press—but now that I've got your attention, here's what you need to know about DOS:

Files and Directories, Oh My!

DOS stores information in *files*. Anything can be placed in a file: a memo, a budget report, or even a graphics image (like a picture of a boat or a computer). You use *directories* to organize your files. Think of a directory as a drawer in a large file cabinet: you can keep your files in whatever drawers (directories) you want.

The letter you see in the DOS prompt represents the disk drive you're working on (for example, C). The letter C refers to the hard drive, and the letters A and B refer to diskette drives. To change to another disk drive (such as drive A):

1. Type **drive:**.

2. Press ⏎Enter.

Make sure to type a colon (:) not a semicolon (;). Doesn't this remind you of your high school English class? We got extra points for semicolons; it was fun thinking up ways to insert them; hey, it got me an A! Well, no extra points here: to change drives, type the drive letter, followed by a *colon*.

Try This!

For example, type **A:** and press **Enter** to change to the A drive. By the way, it's best to actually have something in drive A (such as, say, a diskette) before you try to change to drive A. If you don't, then DOS will give you an error message, and you don't want one of those, do you? (If you get an error message when changing to a drive, insert your diskette or CD-ROM or whatever, then press Ⓡ for retry.)

When you have changed drives, the prompt changes to let you know this world-shattering fact. If you change to drive A, your prompt might look like this:

    A>

or something like this:

    A:\>

If you change back to drive C, you might see something like this:

    C:\DOS>

The **\DOS** in this prompt (C:\DOS>) tells you what directory you're working in. Both of these things are important, because DOS *only works* on the files in the current directory and drive. Oops! So if, for example, you want to delete files in your \PROJECT directory and not \DOS, you need to change directories first:

1. Type **CD**.

2. Type the name of the directory to change to.

3. Press ⏎Enter.

Try This!

For example, to change to the PROJECTS directory, type **CD\PROJECTS** and press ⏎Enter. Now that you're safely in the \PROJECTS directory, you can use the DEL command to delete those files you wanted to get rid of.

Actually, you can make DOS "do" files in other directories, by including a *file path* in your command. If you're curious, beat a path to "Why Entering a File Path Saves You Time and Hassle," later in this section.

Setting Up a PATH for DOS to Follow

There are two types of DOS commands: *internal* and *external*. Internal DOS commands are always available, like a 24-hour cash machine. This means that when you type an internal command such as DIR, it works. External DOS commands are not always available. They're like your bank which, because it uses real people who have a life outside of work (imagine that), is only open between the hours of 3 and 4 on Tuesdays and Thursdays, in months ending in R. This means that you could be happily working with DOS, and one day you could type something like FORMAT, and it wouldn't work. Bummer. But hold on, that's not all! External commands *will* work if:

> ➤ You are in the DOS directory. (How do you get there? Use the CD command.)

> OR

> ➤ You set up a DOS path. (How do you set up this path? Well, read on...)

The easiest way to make all DOS commands (both internal and external) available all the time is to set up a DOS path. A *DOS path* is a listing of directories that DOS should check before it gives you a Bad command or file name message, meaning it can't find the command you just typed. If you set up a DOS path, then DOS can find where the external commands are hiding, and it won't give you that error message when you ask for one of the external commands.

How do you know if you've got a DOS path? Well, type this:

PATH

and press ⏎Enter. If you see No Path, then you don't have one. Go directly to jail and do not pass Go. If you see a bunch of directories listed, make sure you see C:\DOS in the list somewhere. If you do, you're OK, and you can skip on down to the next heading in this section.

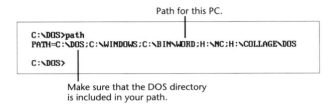

Path for this PC.

```
C:\DOS>path
PATH=C:\DOS;C:\WINDOWS;C:\BIN\WORD;H:\MC;H:\COLLAGE\DOS

C:\DOS>
```

Make sure that the DOS directory
is included in your path.

If you don't have a path, or if your path doesn't include
the DOS directory (C:\DOS), you need to set up a path
so you can use the external DOS commands. For a
guaranteed path when you need it, add this command to
your AUTOEXEC.BAT (for more help, see "More Than
You'll Want to Know About Configuring Your PC," later
in this book):

PATH=C:\DOS

This translates as "Set up a search path to drive C, to a
directory called \DOS." That's it. Now your external DOS
commands are available 24 hours a day, regardless of
which directory you are in.

Getting Help When You Need It

If you are using *at least* DOS version 5 (see "What's Your
DOS Version?" a few pages back on how to figure out
what DOS version you have), you can get instant help
on any command by typing **HELP**. For example, to get
help on the COPY command, type this:

1. Type **COPY**.

2. Press [Spacebar].

3. Type /?.

4. Press [⏎Enter].

Alternatively, you can type this:

1. Type **HELP**.

2. Press [Spacebar].

3. Type **COPY**.

4. Press (⏎Enter).

Click here to find helpful notes and examples.

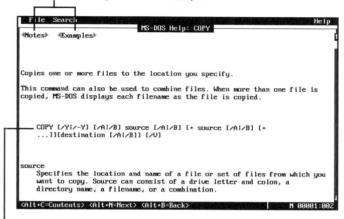

Stay away from confusing syntax!

When you access Help, you'll be greeted with some confusing syntax that only makes sense when you're already familiar with a command. To learn about new commands so you can decipher what Help is trying to tell you, or to get the most help out of Help, see the DOS Command Reference section.

Shelling Out

If you were raised on ATMs, music videos, and movies like *Jurassic Park* and *Terminator 2*, then the DOS prompt will probably bore you to tears with its lack of sophistication. If you yearn for a DOS universe in color, click your heels three times and try the DOS Shell. It'll make using DOS *almost fun*. See the special section on the DOS Shell later in the book.

Things You Should Know About Entering DOS Commands

Well, it's almost graduation day here at DOS High, but you need to know just a few more things before you enter the world of DOS:

How to Make Things Happen

You can type anything you want at the DOS prompt, but until you press Enter, nothing happens. That's why pressing Enter is always included as one of the steps for each command.

A Capital Idea

Forget what Mrs. Haperston taught you—with DOS, capitalization just doesn't matter. Use caps or don't; DOS gives all characters equal rights. Most computer books (including this one) show DOS commands in capital letters, as in TIME. I type my commands in capital letters, so I can see what I'm doing. But lowercase commands are fine too.

Parameter Paranoia and How to Get Over It

Parameters tell a DOS command which files, directories, or drives to work with. For example, you can type **DIR HARD2FND.DOC** to get the DIR command to search for and list the specific file HARD2FND.DOC. You can type **DIR A:** to get the DIR command to list only the files on drive A. Parameters tell a command such as DIR which drives, directories, or files you want the command to use (if any).

In this book, parameters are listed in *italics*, because you have to substitute a bit of reality for them:

1. Type **DIR**.

2. Press ⌷ Spacebar ⌷.

3. Type the name of a file (like this: *filename*).

4. Press ⌐Enter⌐.

You substitute a real name for the word *filename* in step 3. What you'd really type is:

DIR LOSTFILE.DOC

Why Entering a File Path Saves You Time and Hassle

When you enter a DOS command, it acts upon the files in the current directory. If you are in the \WINDOWS directory when you enter the DEL (delete) command, you'll end up deleting files in the \WINDOWS directory. Hint: this is really not a good thing to do.

To let the DOS command know that you're the one in charge here, you can provide a *file path* (a listing which describes the exact route that DOS should take to find the files you want it to use with the command) along with the DOS command when you enter it. It's a lot more typing to include a file path with the DEL command, but it's a lot less trouble than jumping back and forth between directories just so DOS can find the files you want to delete!

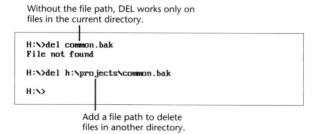

Without the file path, DEL works only on files in the current directory.

```
H:\>del common.bak
File not found

H:\>del h:\projects\common.bak

H:\>
```

Add a file path to delete files in another directory.

A file path consists of three parts:

➤ The drive the file is located on followed by a colon, as in C:.

➤ A *backslash* (\) followed by the complete directory path to the file. Start with the parent directory, then add another backslash, and a subdirectory name if applicable. Finish up with a final backslash, as in \123\WORK\.

➤ End the path name with a filename or file specification, as in OLD.WK4.

The completed path would look like this:

    C:\123\WORK\OLD.WK4

To delete the OLD.WK4 file, you'd type DEL C:\123\WORK\OLD.WK4. That's DEL, then space, followed by the file path. With the file path included with the DEL command, DOS knows to delete the OLD.WK4 file in the \123\WORK directory on the C drive, and to not go wild, deleting files in whatever directory you happen to be wandering through.

Those Darn Slashes

You should get to know the difference between the forward slash (/) and the backslash (\). The forward slash is used to designate a *switch*, a part of a DOS command that overrides what that command normally does. For example, if you type just type

    DIR

you'll get a listing of files in the current directory, running down the screen. But if you type

    DIR /W

the files are displayed across the screen instead of downward. *The forward slash indicates the use of a switch*—in this case, /**W**, which means wide display.

The backslash is used in *path names*, to designate a directory, as in

    C:\DOS

A *path* is the route that DOS travels from the root directory to any subdirectories when locating a file. Think of telling a friend how to find your house. A complete path name looks like this:

    C:\WORD\DOCS\CHAP01.DOC

In this case, the backslash separates the disk drive name C: from the directory name DOCS. A backslash is also used within a path name to separate a directory name from a filename. For example:

    C:\WORD\CHAP10.DOC

In this case, the backslash separates the disk drive name C: from the directory name WORD, which is separated from the *filename*, CHAP10.DOC.

Getting Wild

You can specify more than one file for a command to work with, simply by using wildcards. A DOS *wildcard* is just like the wild cards in card games, where you can substitute a "wild" Joker or deuce for the Queen of Spades or whatever card you need to win. In a similar fashion, a DOS wildcard represents a character or characters within a filename. Wildcards create a general filename *pattern* so that several files can be used with a single DOS command. There are two DOS wildcards: the asterisk (*) and the question mark (?).

> **The asterisk (*)** is kind of like having a whole handful of wildcards. The single * represents several characters within a filename. For example, *.DOC means "use files that have any first name, but a last name of DOC." Using K*.DOC means "use files that begin with K, followed by a bunch of miscellaneous characters, and have a last name of DOC. Using *.* means "use files with any first or last name," in other words, "use all the files." *DOS ignores any characters after an asterisk*, so M*RCH.* is the same as M*.*.

The question mark (?) represents a single character within a filename. For example, JO?N.WKS means "use files that begin with the letters JO, followed by any single character, followed by an N, and the extension .WKS." The files JOHN.WKS and JOAN.WKS match this pattern, but the files JEAN.WKS and JOHNNY.WKS do not. You can use additional question marks to represent other characters, as in JO??.WKS, but the number of characters must also match. The files JOHN.WKS, JOKE.WKS and JOAN.WKS would match this filename pattern, but JOKES.WKS would not because it has five characters in its first name.

You can have lots of fun with wildcards. For example, instead of deleting a single file, you can arrange your own private electronic bonfire by typing **DEL 1993*.*** (Poof! There go the files in the 1993 directory. Somebody pass the marshmallows.)

Repeating Yourself

If you're issuing the same DOS command over and over again, you may find that typing it over and over becomes tedious. For example, if you're examining the contents of one diskette after another, you might be typing the following command repeatedly:

DIR A:

The A: tells the DIR command to list the files on the diskette in drive A.

Instead of retyping the command every time you insert a different diskette in drive A, simply press F3.

You'll see the command redisplayed as if you had really typed it (David Copperfield, eat your heart out):

DIR A:

Press ⏎Enter to execute the command, and you're on your way!

If you find yourself using the same commands over and over in a kind of DOS deja vu, install DOSKEY and let it recall past commands for you so you don't have to retype them. See DOSKEY in the DOS Command Reference section.

To Err Is Common: What to Do if You Type a Mistake

If you type a mistake *before you press Enter*, try one of these to correct it:

> **Press the** ⟨⬅Backspace⟩ **key.** Back up and erase the incorrect characters, and retype them.

> **Press the** ⟨Esc⟩ **key.** This will erase the entire line, and let you start over. On most computers, when you press ⟨Esc⟩, you will see a backslash (\), and the cursor will move down one line. Type your command there. If you feel nervous about typing a command without the DOS prompt, press ⟨⏎Enter⟩ after pressing ⟨Esc⟩.

> Dorothy, you're back in Kansas.

If you've already pressed Enter (you quick-fingered person, you), then try one of these:

> **Press Ctrl+Break.** Hold down the ⟨Ctrl⟩ key while you press the ⟨Break⟩ key. It works like Esc, but will return you to a nice friendly DOS prompt. You can also cancel some commands with Ctrl+Break *after you press Enter* (after they've started running). If you can't find the Break key, use ⟨Ctrl⟩ + ⟨C⟩ instead.

> **Repeat the command and correct it so that this time, it works.** If you pressed Enter but got an error message because you mistyped the command, repeat the command by pressing ⟨F3⟩. Then use the

arrow keys to position the cursor where you'd like to insert or delete characters, Once you have the cursor positioned, press any character, and it's inserted at that spot. To delete an extra character, press (Del). Once the command is correctly typed, press (↩Enter) again.

If you see an error message, check out the error message help section in the back of this pocket reference. (This reference is soooo handy, don't you wish you had two, one for each pocket?)

Making Friends with a Mouse

Some of the newer DOS commands present you with cool graphics from which you can choose what you want to do by using your mouse. This makes DOS almost modern, but the effect is more like your grandfather wearing grunge. Anyway, it's nice that DOS recognizes that you have a mouse, even if it's only once in a while.

You don't have to use a mouse at all with DOS, but when you're using the DOS Shell, MSBACKUP, DRVSPACE, EDIT, and some other utilities, it'll be far easier than sticking to the keyboard. Here's the basics you need to know to use little Mickey:

To use the mouse, you either *click* or *double-click* with the left mouse button. Some actions require that you *drag* the mouse (no, not along the floor—along the mouse pad!).

➤ **Point** You use the mouse to issue commands by pointing at something on-screen, such as a menu, or an icon (a tiny picture which represents something such as a file). To point with the mouse (I know, your mother always said it was impolite to point, but here it's OK) drag the mouse along the mouse pad in the direction you want the mouse pointer (the little arrow thingy) to go. For example, to point at something at the top of your screen, drag the mouse up, towards the top of the mouse pad.

If you run out of mouse pad, what do you do? Easy—
just pick the thing up and set it back down in the
middle of the pad. The mouse pointer on-screen will
not be affected in the least.

➤ **Click**   To click with the mouse, press the mouse
button once. You click to select something, such as
a menu, to open it. Once the menu is open, click
on a command to select it.

➤ **Double-click**   To double-click with the mouse,
press the mouse button twice in rapid succession.

➤ **Drag**   To drag with the mouse, first move the
mouse pointer to the starting position. Now click
and hold the mouse button. Drag the mouse
pointer to the ending position, and then release
the mouse button. You might drag to select several
files in the DOS Shell or MSBACKUP.

In this section you've learned about DOS commands,
DOS utilities, and the DOS prompt. In the next sections,
you'll learn about each individual DOS command, and
the utility programs included with DOS 6.2.

Bossing DOS: A DOS Command Reference

ANSI.SYS

ANSI.SYS is a device driver (it "drives" or manages a "device," in this case your monitor, making it behave a certain way). Used in the CONFIG.SYS file, ANSI.SYS makes it possible for programs to access the extended DOS character set, whatever that is. Some old-style programs need ANSI.SYS so they can display boxes and buttons and pretty graphical menus on your screen. There are pathetically few programs still out there that actually require access to ANSI.SYS, so don't bother adding this line to your CONFIG.SYS—unless you try running some program and it demands the line with a message such as, "ANSI.SYS must be installed to perform requested function."

See the section, "Hacking Away at Files With the DOS Editor" later in this book for steps on hacking up (I mean "editing") your CONFIG.SYS.

On a new line near the beginning of your CONFIG.SYS file:

1. Type **DEVICE=C:\DOS\ANSI.SYS**

2. Save the CONFIG.SYS file:

   Click on **File**, click on **Exit**, and click on **Yes**.

3. Reboot your PC so the command can take effect by pressing (Ctrl) + (Alt) + (Del).

For more info on ANSI.SYS, see *The Complete Idiot's Guide to DOS*, Chapter 17, "AUTOEXEC.BAT, CONFIG.SYS, and Other Secret Code Words."

APPEND

APPEND tells DOS to lay off on the "File not found" message whenever you have the nerve to refer to data files that aren't in the current directory. The PATH command works in a similar manner, except it locates programs and DOS commands, whereas APPEND locates data files (the files that *really* count—i.e., they hold your work).

APPEND does not locate data files when you use the DIR or DEL commands (bummer), but it does work with the COPY or MOVE commands (cool). For example, you could APPEND your favorite directory \MYSTUFF to DOS' normal search list, and then whenever you type something like: MOVE GOT2HAVE.IT \SECRET, DOS will obediently move your file from \MYSTUFF to \SECRET without so much as a peep—even though you weren't anywhere near the \MYSTUFF directory at the time. (Hint: without APPEND helping out, you'd have to type this nonsense instead:

```
MOVE C:\MYSTUFF\GOT2HAVE.IT C:\SECRET.
```

Yech. Or you'd have to change directories to \MYSTUFF, do your move, then change back to the directory in which you were working before you were so rudely interrupted by a stupid operating system.)

DO NOT USE the APPEND command if you plan on using Windows. It's a big-time no-no.

APPEND: Adding a Directory to the Search List

To append a directory to the search list (so DOS will search that directory to find a file used in a command before issuing an error message):

1. Type **APPEND**.

2. Press [Spacebar].

3. Type the drive and directory you want to attach (like this: *drive:\directory*).

4. Press [Spacebar].

5. Type */X:ON*.

6. Press [↵Enter].

For example, to append a directory called FILES to the current DOS search list, type **APPEND C:\FILES /X:ON**. Then you could type COPY MYFILE.DOC A: and not get an error message, even though MYFILE.DOC is located in the \FILES directory, and *not the current one*. Way cool.

You can double your pleasure, double your fun by appending more than one directory at a time—just separate them with semicolons (;). For example:

```
APPEND C:\FILES;C:\EXTRADIR
```

APPEND: Canceling the Search List

The following steps remove all of the appended directories from the search list:

1. Type **APPEND**.
2. Press [Spacebar].
3. Type ; .
4. Press [⏎Enter].

ATTRIB

ATTRIB enables you to change the attributes (characteristics) of a file. (If only changing your own attributes—such as losing a few inches around the middle—were as easy!)

Attribute	Abbreviation	Meaning
Read-Only	r	File cannot be changed.
Archive	a	File has been changed since backup.
Hidden	h	File is hidden from normal file listings.
System	s	File is used for MS-DOS system operations.

Be a Scrooge (i.e. extremely miserly) when it comes to this command, and don't use it unless you have to. Most files are set to read-only, archive, hidden, or system for a reason; playing around with ATTRIB without knowing those reasons might lead you and Curious George right into big-time trouble.

ATTRIB: Displaying Attributes

To display a file's attributes:

1. Type **ATTRIB**.

2. Press [Spacebar].

3. Type the filename (like this: *filename.ext*).

4. Press [↵Enter].

For example, to see the attributes of the file,
WORD.EXE, don't use a crystal ball—just type **ATTRIB**
WORD.EXE.

ATTRIB: Changing File Attributes

To change a file's attributes:

1. Type **ATTRIB**.

2. Press [Spacebar].

3. Type **+** or **–** to add or delete an attribute.

4. Type the attribute's abbreviation (see the table at
   the beginning of the ATTRIB section).

5. Press [Spacebar].

6. Type the filename (like this: *filename.ext*).

7. Press [↵Enter].

For example, to remove the read-only attribute from
TEXTFILE.DOC so you can delete the file (even
though somebody thought they could stop you by
being cute and turning on the read-only attribute in
the first place), type **ATTRIB -r TEXTFILE.DOC**. Then
type your **DEL** command. Ha! That'll show 'em.

If you add an /S switch at the end, ATTRIB acts on all subdirectories under the current directory. So to prevent ol' Ralph from messing up your files while you're on vacation, type **ATTRIB +r C:\PRIVATE /S**. The little /S addition will set all the files in C:\PRIVATE (plus any subdirectories of C:\PRIVATE) to read-only, so they can't be changed. When you come back from vacation, type **ATTRIB -r C:\PRIVATE /S** to unlock 'em.

BREAK

When a program or a command does something bizarre, you may feel like throwing your hands up and shouting, "Give me a break!" Well, you don't have to shout in vain; instead, you can give the errant program or command a "break" by pressing one of the Break key combinations: Ctrl + Break or Ctrl + C.

But Ctrl + Break may not have an immediate effect; a program usually waits until it receives input or gives output before it finally notices that you asked it to stop. If this nonchalant attitude perturbs you, you can set BREAK to ON, and force programs to pay better attention. Here's how:

1. Type **BREAK**.

2. Press Spacebar.

3. Type **ON**.

4. Press ↵Enter.

Add the BREAK command to your CONFIG.SYS file, so your programs will always hear you when you shout. (Now if it could only do the same with your kids.)

To turn BREAK off, type **BREAK OFF**. Turning BREAK off is useful when you notice that your programs have slowed down considerably because now that they're paying so much attention to you, they're not paying enough attention to what they're doing.

BUFFERS

BUFFERS is a command that goes in your CONFIG.SYS file. Buffers increase your PC's efficiency by storing frequently requested files in a handy spot in memory (RAM). With buffers, the PC doesn't have to go all the way back to the hard disk to get a file whenever a program needs it—it can just wallow on the couch and reach over to the old buffer area instead. Buffers decrease the amount of time it takes for the PC to get stuff done, thereby increasing the amount of things you can accomplish before you decide it's time to call it a day (on bad days, for me, this is about 9:00 a.m.).

Most programs have a minimum number of buffers they need for peak performance. A database program may require 20 to 30 buffers, while a word processor may only need 10 to 15. When needs conflict, use a number that's high enough to accommodate everyone. In this example, you might select 25 (it's not too high and not too low, and should make both the database and word processor happy as pigeons).

The BUFFERS command goes in your CONFIG.SYS file. Typing this command at the DOS prompt does nothing but amuse nerds who know better, but don't mind seeing someone else try in vain to use the command that way.

When you're ready to try this command in your CONFIG.SYS file, get out your Ginsu knife and read the section, "Hacking Away at Files With the DOS Editor" later in this book, for more information.

On a new line near the beginning of your CONFIG.SYS file:

1. Type **BUFFERS=**.

2. Type the number of buffers desired.

A common number to use is 30. For example, you might type **BUFFERS=30**. Very few programs ever need more than 50. Check the documentation for your programs to find out what you need.

If you're using SMARTDrive (a disk cache), it's best to use only 10 buffers or less. If you use more than that, you may need to take some BUFFER-in, because you won't see any speed increase at all—what you will see is a decrease in memory, a valuable PC resource you shouldn't go around wasting.

If you load DOS into high memory (see the DOS command) and you're using DriveSpace (a utility which magically doubles the space on your hard disk—read all about it in this section), you should also use only 10 buffers or less. Using more wastes memory, which as I said before, is a bad thing.

For more info on BUFFERS and other padded objects, see *The Complete Idiot's Guide to DOS*, Chapter 17, "AUTOEXEC.BAT, CONFIG.SYS, and Other Secret Code Words."

CD (CHDIR)

You gotta love a command with only two letters. CD changes the current (active) directory. If you must type as much as possible in order to flaunt the one thing you learned in high school that you still remember (typing class), use CHDIR.

For more info on CD, see *The Complete Idiot's Guide to DOS*, Chapter 7, "Navigating the DOS Jungle of Files and Directories."

CD: Changing Directories

To change directories:

1. Type **CD**.

2. Type the name of the directory.

3. Press (↵Enter).

Try This!

For example, to change to the DATA directory, type **CD\DATA**. To change your mind, see your psychiatrist.

If you are changing to a directory that is directly *below* the current one, you can substitute a space for the backslash (\); for example, to change from C:\WORD to C:\WORD\PROJECTS, typing **CD PROJECTS** saves wear and tear on your dainty digits, and works the same as typing **CD\WORD\PROJECTS**.

To change to the directory *above* the current one, type **CD..** For example, typing **CD..** from the \WORD\PROJECTS directory takes you directly to the \WORD directory, thank you very much.

By the way, all this changing can get a person mighty confused as to where on the darn disk they might be. Change your prompt command so it always tells you.

(Either that, or carry a map.) See PROMPT later in this section.

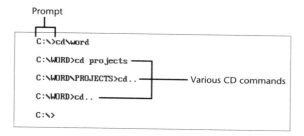

Prompt

```
C:\>cd\word

C:\WORD>cd projects ──────┐
                          │
C:\WORD\PROJECTS>cd.. ·────┼──── Various CD commands
                          │
C:\WORD>cd.. ─────────────┘

C:\>
```

CD: Returning to the Root Directory

The *root directory* is another name for the top directory or the "lobby" of the disk. To return to the root directory:

1. Type **CD**\.

2. Press ⏎Enter.

CHKDSK

Although DOS 6.2 comes with CHKDSK (probably put there just to confuse you), you should use SCANDISK instead. See SCANDISK later in this section.

If you're feeling nostalgic, you can read more about old CHKDSK. See *The Complete Idiot's Guide to DOS*, Chapter 5, "Becoming a Disk Jockey."

CHOICE

In a free and democratic society, there should always be a choice: in the Presidential elections, for example, there is often a choice between Mr. Bozo and Mr. I-Can't-Believe-I'm-Voting-For-This-Jerk-But At-Least-He's-Not-As-Bad-As-Mr.-Bozo. DOS supports this time-honored tradition by allowing you to place choices in your batch files—for example, the AUTOEXEC.BAT.

To learn how to edit your AUTOEXEC.BAT, see the section, "Hacking Away at Files With the DOS Editor." To learn how to turn a horrible act into a money-making machine, see "How to Whack Your Enemies, Get Caught, and Still Profit By Going on TV in Japan" by Tonya Harding.

On a line in a batch file (such as the AUTOEXEC.BAT):

1. Type **CHOICE**.

2. Press ⎡ Spacebar ⎤.

3. **(Optional)** Enter the keys to use as choices: **/C:*keykeykey*** and press ⎡ Spacebar ⎤. (You can have any number of keys, not just three—just make sure not to insert any commas or spaces between the keys.)

For example, to have the user press C to continue with the batch file, or G to Get the heck out of there, type **/C:CG**. If you choose not to specify anything, then the choices the user sees are a boring Y or N.

4. **(Optional)** Enter the default choice, which is the key letter plus the number of seconds you want the system to wait before the default goes into effect. Type **/T:*key,nn*** and press ⎡ Spacebar ⎤.

To have CHOICE wait five seconds before defaulting to choice C (for "Come on, let's get on with it"), type **/T:C,5**.

5. **(Optional)** Type the text you want CHOICE to display.

Okay, for those of you who got a little lost in the preceding steps (what a mess of options, eh?), here's an example. To have CHOICE display the message

```
Give up now, or suffer brutal defeat later?[N,L]?
```

type **CHOICE /C:N,L Give up now, or suffer brutal defeat later?**

To figure out which choice the user makes, there's no ands or buts about it—you should use the IF command in your batch file. If the user chooses the first choice (such as C for Continue), then ERRORLEVEL=1. So you could use the IF command in your batch file by including something like, **IF ERRORLEVEL=1 GOTO CONTINUE**. You can test to see if user chose door number 2 instead by including the command, **IF ERRORLEVEL=2 GOTO DOORTWO** or somesuch in your batch file.

Still confused? There's an example in the following figure. But if you still don't figure, don't feel bad. Batch files aren't for everyone. Lots of people live their entire lives very happily without writing one. (Really!) If you're determined to learn more about batch files, however, see commands such as ECHO, FOR, GOTO, IF, PAUSE, and REM for more information. If you're truly a glutton for punishment (or just desperate) type **HELP BATCH** at the DOS prompt.

```
   File  Edit  Search  Options                              Help
┌──────────────────────────┤ DELFILES.BAT ├──────────────────────┐
│@ECHO OFF                                                        ▲│
│REM This batch file removes old .bak files from the hard disk.   │
│CLS                                                              ║│
│ECHO.                                                            ║│
│ECHO.                                                            ║│
│DIR C:\PROJECTS\*.BAK /P                                         ║│
│ECHO.                                                            ║│
│PAUSE                                                            ║│
│CLS                                                             ▓▓│
│CHOICE /C:CG /T:C,5 Continue with delete, or Give up?            │
│IF ERRORLEVEL 2 GOTO END                                         │
│DEL C:\PROJECTS\*.BAK                                            │
│ECHO Done! Those files are gonners!                              │
│:END                                                             │
│                                                                ▼│
│◄▓▓▓▓▓▓▓▓▓▓▓▓▓▓▓▓▓▓▓▓▓▓▓▓▓▓▓▓▓▓▓▓▓▓▓▓▓▓▓▓▓▓▓▓▓▓▓▓▓▓▓▓▓▓▓▓▓▓►│
│ MS-DOS Editor  <F1=Help> Press ALT to activate menus            │
└─────────────────────────────────────────────────────────────────┘
```

Sample batch file gives you a choice

CLS

CLS clears the screen of bugs, tar, and other stuff kicked up by your DOS commmnds. It's also good for removing error messages from your screen so you can pretend they never happened.

1. Type **CLS**.

2. Press ⎡←Enter⎤.

COPY

Copy from a neighbor in school, and you get an "F" and a free trip to the principal's office. Copy files in DOS, and you get a duplicate file, stashed in another directory or drive, with the same or a different name. Beats Mr. Hardcase's office anytime.

If you should make the faux pas of all faux pas by trying to copy a file on top of another version of itself, COPY asks for confirmation. (Actually, you may very well want to overwrite an older version of a file with a newer copy.) If confronted with such a warning, press **Y** to continue with the COPY, or **N** to abort in shame. By the way, COPY does *not* ask for confirmation if you use the command in a batch file.

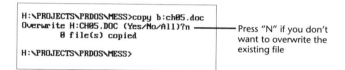

```
H:\PROJECTS\PRDOS\MESS>copy b:ch05.doc
Overwrite H:CH05.DOC (Yes/No/All)?n
     0 file(s) copied

H:\PROJECTS\PRDOS\MESS>
```
— Press "N" if you don't want to overwrite the existing file

For more on COPY than you might ever need, see *The Complete Idiot's Guide to DOS*, Chapter 11, "Standing at the Copier, Copying Files."

COPY: Creating a Duplicate File

To create a duplicate of a file in the same directory, follow these steps:

1. Type **COPY**.

2. Press [Spacebar].

3. Type the file to copy (like this: ***filename.ext***).

4. Press [Spacebar].

5. Type the name for the new copy (like this: ***filename.ext***).

6. Press [↵Enter].

Try This!

For example, if you type **COPY REPORT.DOC BACKUP.DOC**, DOS makes a copy of REPORT.DOC, calls it BACKUP.DOC, and places it in the same directory as REPORT.DOC, unless of course, it does something else (just kidding).

COPY: Creating a Duplicate in Another Directory

To create a duplicate of a file (with the same or a different name) in a different directory, you can simply follow these steps. But before you do, let me share some of my infinite wisdom on the subject. (OK, it might not be so wise, but it'll save you time, so isn't that worth the few minutes it'll take to read it?)

Anyway, you can get wild and copy multiple files at the same time by using wildcards. For example, to copy all .DOC files in the current directory to the \WILD directory, type **COPY *.DOC C:\WILD**. See the earlier section, "The Least You Need to Know About DOS" for a wild time with wildcards.

Be aware that COPY normally copies only files in the current directory. So let your fingers do the walking with a file *path*, which enables you to copy files *not* in the current directory. See "The Least You Need to Know About DOS" for the least you need to know.

1. Type **COPY**.

2. Press [Spacebar].

3. Type the file to copy *filename.ext*.

4. Press [Spacebar].

5. Type the destination *drive:\directory*.

For example, if you type **COPY MESS.WK4 A:** you'll copy your financial worksheet onto a diskette so you can take it to your accountant to fix (maybe you can persuade him to make a small donation to balance the numbers).

6. **(Optional)** Type a new name for the copy (like this: *filename.ext*).

7. Press ⏎Enter.

Tip

If you skip step 6, the copy will have the same name as the original. But if that bothers you, you can think of the copy as "new and improved." After all, that's how they sell the same kind of soap, etc. year after year.

Adding a /V switch at the end of the COPY command causes it to switch to "Schwarzenegger" mode, where files that aren't copied properly are terminated, then redone.

DATE

Produces a tall blond for a last-minute rendevous. (Just kidding—but who knows? This may show up in a new version of DOS.) Actually, this command allows you to change or display the computer's date.

For a longer date with the DATE command, see *The Complete Idiot's Guide to DOS*, Chapter 3, "Gentlemen and Ladies, Start Your PCs."

DATE: Displaying the Date

1. Type **DATE**.
2. Press ⏎Enter.

DATE: Changing the Date

1. Type **DATE**.
2. Press ⏎Enter.
3. Type the new date *mm-dd-yy* (two characters each for month, day, and year).

For you nonconformists, you can also type the date with slashes, as in 10/16/95. For real weirdness, you can type it with periods, as in 10.16.95.

4. Press ⏎Enter.

DBLSPACE

In the tradition of big corporations that don't always explain why they do what they do, Microsoft changed the name of DoubleSpace to DriveSpace in DOS version 6.22. Who cares why, since DriveSpace works basically the same way DoubleSpace did? So if you're still operating with yesterday's model (DoubleSpace) skip over to DRVSPACE, where you'll find the particulars on how to operate your classic.

OK, so you dragged it out of me—the reason that Microsoft changed the name of DoubleSpace is because they ran into a legal disagreement and took it out of DOS 6.21. In the new DOS 6.22, DoubleSpace was replaced by DriveSpace, probably so that everyone would forget the whole mess as quickly as possible. Anyway, DriveSpace looks and acts the same as DoubleSpace to you, the user, so like, who cares?

If you've got DoubleSpace and it intends to stay, check out *The Complete Idiot's Guide to DOS*, Chapter 19, "Double Your Pleasure, Double Your Fun, Double Your Disk."

DEFRAG

DEFRAG is a utility that tidies up the way files are organized on your hard disk.

If you're dying for more info on DEFRAG, see *The Complete Idiot's Guide to DOS*, Chapter 5, "Becoming a Disk Jockey."

DEFRAG: What Is It?

DOS will never make Housekeeper of the Year, because it's downright sloppy when it comes to keeping files organized on your hard disk. You see, when your hard disk is all new and shiny, files are broken into small pieces and placed in nice, neat rows, right next to each other. But as you make changes to files, delete them, or copy new ones, this pretty picture starts to look as organized as a teenager's closet, with those file pieces thrown into any convenient corner. In techno-speak, your files are "fragmented."

As fragmentation gets worse, it takes longer and longer for DOS to find all the pieces to a file. DEFRAG whisks through, putting all the pieces of each Humpty Dumpty file back together again on the disk ("defragmenting" the files). And great news! This nice, neat picture will last as long as you don't do anything on your PC. Because as soon as you do, DOS starts placing files hither and yon, scattering the pieces willy-nilly over the hard disk. So run DEFRAG once a month or so to fix this problem.

Warning! Defragmenting may take an hour or so, so you might want to start DEFRAG late in the day, and not right before an important meeting with (say) the IRS. Not that the IRS doesn't have a sense of humor, but they might not like it if you say you don't have access to your accounting records right now because you're "defragging."

A few "by the ways" before you start. First, if you're using DoubleSpace or DriveSpace, skip to the DRVSPACE section for details on defragging your drive. Also, you can't use DEFRAG on a network drive, so don't even try. Also, if you use Windows or the DOS Shell, exit those programs (actually, exit *all programs*) before you start DEFRAG.

DEFRAG: Defragmenting a Hard Drive the Easy Way

1. Type **DEFRAG**.

2. Press [Spacebar].

3. Enter the drive to defragment (such as C) and a colon (:).

For example, to defragment drive C, type (surprise, surprise) **DEFRAG C:**.

4. Press [↵Enter].

After step 4, DEFRAG analyzes your hard disk and recommends the best procedure for defragging. If it says that your hard disk is pretty much "optimized," then just skip the whole thing: press [Esc] and click on **Exit**.

Otherwise continue with the steps.

5. If you're ready to optimize, click on **Optimize**.

6. Wait for the defragmenting process to finish.

7. When you get the message Optimization complete, click on **Exit**. You're outta there.

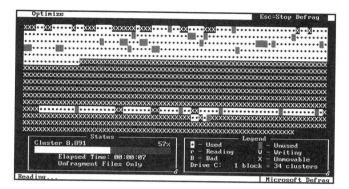

DEFRAG: Defragmenting a Hard Drive the Macho Way

By not accepting DEFRAG's default settings, you can customize the way DEFRAG works. Here's how to defragment a hard drive the macho (hard) way:

1. Type **DEFRAG**.

2. Press ⌷ Spacebar ⌷.

3. Enter the drive to defragment (such as **C**) and a colon (:).

4. Press ⌷Enter⌷

5. Click on **Configure**.

6. (Optional) Click on **Optimization Method**. Choose a method, then click on **OK**.

7. (Optional) Click on **File Sort**. Select a sort criterion, a sort order, then click on **OK**.

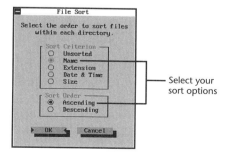

Select your
sort options

8. Click on **Begin Optimization**.

9. Wait for the defragmenting process to finish.

Now's a good time to do the laundry or some such, because defragmenting takes awhile.

10. When you see Optimization complete, Click on **Exit**.

DEL (ERASE)

You use your PC to create things such as memos, reports, charts, and analyses—and there they sit, on your hard disk, long after they've outlived their usefulness. (Some files just never know when to leave a party.) With the DEL command, you can clean out those old dust-bunny files you no longer need. Gotta do this manually; sorry, but there's no way to train your PC to take out the garbage.

Okay, they are different names, but they do the same thing. Use DEL, DELETE, or ERASE, whichever you prefer. It's a free country.

If you get gung-ho and delete an important file, don't worry about losing your job. Just see the UNDELETE genie to make a little magic.

For more info on DEL, see *The Complete Idiot's Guide to DOS*, Chapter 12, "Spring Cleaning—Deleting Unwanted Files."

DEL: Deleting a Single File in the Current Directory

1. Type **DEL**.

2. Press [Spacebar].

3. Type the file name (like this: *filename.ext*).

4. Press [↵Enter].

If the file to be deleted isn't in the current directory, you must change to that directory first (see the CD command) or type the file's drive and directory before its name. For example, from the C: drive, you might type:

DEL A:\JUNK\GOTTAGO.DOC.

DEL: Deleting Multiple Files

To delete multiple files, you use wildcards: * or ?. (See the section "The Least You Need to Know About DOS" for the lowdown on wildcard wizardry.) To delete multiple files in the current directory:

1. Type **DEL**.

2. Press [Spacebar].

3. Type a file pattern using wildcards (? or *).

4. Press [↵Enter].

Here are some examples: To delete all files with a .BAK extension, type **DEL *.BAK**. To delete all files in the directory, type **DEL *.***. To delete all files that begin with M and have 3 other letters, type **DEL M???.***. To delete an old boyfriend or girlfriend from your address book, use a black marker, extra-wide.

You can have DOS prompt you before it stomps on each file by typing **/P** at the end of the DEL command, like this: **DEL KINDA???.CRP /P**. Then, when asked, press Ⓨ to delete a file, or Ⓝ if you have a change of heart.

DELOLDOS

True to its sloppy Oscar Madison personality, DOS leaves a copy of your old DOS files lying around in a directory called \OLD_DOS.1. This allows you the freedom of returning to the stone knives and bear skins of your older DOS version, should you get hit with a large rock and rendered temporarily crazy. Instead, run DELOLDOS to remove your old DOS files and free up disk space.

1. Type **DELOLDOS**.
2. Press ⏎Enter.
3. Press Ⓨ.

DELTREE

Unlike the wimpy RD command (which requires that you remove any unwanted files yourself), DELTREE gleefully destroys your directories and subdirectories (even if they still contain files).

Be careful; once a directory is removed, you can't bring back from the dead (undelete) the files that were in it.

To remove a directory and all its files and subdirectories:

1. Type **CD**\.

2. Type the name of the directory immediately above the one you want to delete.

3. Press ⏎Enter.

Try This!

For example, if you want to remove C:\WORKS, change to the root directory (type **CD**\), which is one level above it in the directory tree. If you want to remove C:\WORKS\STUFF, type **CD\WORKS** instead.

---

4. Type **DELTREE**.

5. Press ⎵Spacebar⎵.

6. Type the name of the directory to remove.

7. Press ⏎Enter.

8. To confirm, press Y.

9. Press ⏎Enter.

Want more info on DELTREE? Then check out *The Complete Idiot's Guide to DOS*, Chapter 13, "Let Your Fingers Do the Walking—Directory Assistance."

DEVICE

DEVICE installs a device driver into memory. A device driver acts like a combination traffic cop/interpreter/pen knife for data going to and from a foreign device (like a mouse, a printer, a CD-ROM, or a tax accountant). This command works only in the CONFIG.SYS file; you can't type it at the DOS prompt. (Well, okay, you *can* actually type it, but it won't *do* anything, no matter how long you stare at it.)

For the exciting conclusion to the daytime drama, "Editing My CONFIG.SYS File: True Confessions of a Hacker Called Joe," see the real true-life section, "Hacking Away at Files With the DOS Editor" buried at the end of this marvelous book.

On a new line of your CONFIG.SYS file:

1. Type **DEVICE**=.

2. Type the location of the driver file (like this: *drive:\directory*\).

3. Type the name of the driver file (like this: *filename.ext*).

For example, to install the ANSI.SYS device driver into memory, type **DEVICE=C:\DOS\ANSI.SYS**.

For more info on DEVICE and its brother, DEVICEHIGH, see *The Complete Idiot's Guide to DOS*, Chapter 17, "AUTOEXEC.BAT, CONFIG.SYS, and Other Secret Code Words."

DEVICEHIGH

A twin to the DEVICE command, DEVICEHIGH lived in the shadow of its older brother until it was discovered that it had the power to load device drivers into *upper* memory, whatever that is. Just know that this is a good thing because it frees up regular (conventional) memory, which gives you more memory for running programs (instead of silly device drivers). Return-ay-vous to the DEVICE section for actual steps; you use the DEVICEHIGH command exactly like you would the DEVICE command.

DEVICEHIGH may be powerful, but he's nothing without his friends. To get DEVICEHIGH to work, insert the following commands into the CONFIG.SYS before the first DEVICEHIGH line:

> **DEVICE=C:\DOS\HIMEM.SYS**
> **DEVICE=C:\DOS\EMM386.EXE**
> **DOS=HIGH,UMB**

If you're curious about what his friends are up to, refer to the appropriate commands in this section: HIMEM.SYS, EMM386.EXE, and DOS.

DIR

DIR is great for those of us who misplace things on a routine basis, such as our keys, a wallet, or the demo file for the big client meeting which is due to start in five minutes. The DIR command lists files and directories on your PC (provided you ask nicely), enabling you to find your lost file at the last minute and save your reputation.

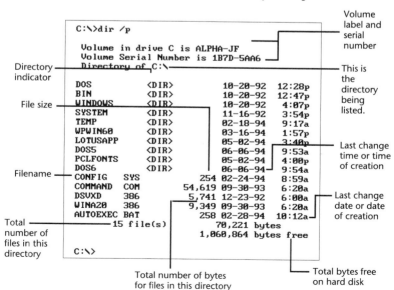

For keys to more DIR enlightenment, read *The Complete Idiot's Guide to DOS*, Chapter 10, "Lost Something? How to Find Files with the DIR Command."

DIR: Listing All Files and Subdirectories in the Current Directory

1. Type **DIR**.
2. Press (↵Enter).

To display the listing one page at a time (so you can read it before it scrolls off into oblivion), add **P** to the command (for example, **DIR/P**). To display a wide listing, use /**W**.

DIR: Listing Only Certain Files in the Current Directory

1. Type **DIR**.
2. Press (Spacebar).
3. Type a file specification.
4. Press (↵Enter).

For example, to see all the files with a .DOC extension, type **DIR *.DOC**. See the section, "The Least You Need to Know About DOS" for directions to the wildcard kingdom.

DIR: Listing Files on Another Drive or in Another Directory

1. Type **DIR**.

2. Press [Spacebar].

3. Type the drive and directory (like this: *drive:\directory*).

Try This!

For example, to list the files on the diskette you've conveniently placed in drive A, type **DIR A:**.

4. **(Optional)** Type a file specification (like this: *filespec*).

5. **(Optional)** To list files in subdirectories too, press [Spacebar], then type **/S**.

6. Press [↵Enter].

DIR: Printing the List of Files

1. Type **DIR**.

2. Press [Spacebar].

3. **(Optional)** Type the drive and directory (like this: *drive:\directory*).

4. **(Optional)** Type a file specification (like this: *filespec*).

5. **(Optional)** If you followed steps 3 and/or 4, press [Spacebar].

6. Direct the output to the printer: **>PRN**.

7. Press [↵Enter].

For example, use **DIR A: >PRN** to print a listing of the
files on a diskette so you can (gasp!) organize them.

DIR: Sorting the Directory Listing

To sort the directory listing in some type of *reasonable*
order such as (dare we think it?) alphabetical:

1. Type **DIR**.

2. Press [Spacebar].

3. Type /O: and then the code for the desired sort
   order:

n	alphabetically by name
-n	reverse alphabetically by name
e	alphabetically by extension
-e	reverse alphabetically by extension
d	by date and time, old to new
-d	by date and time, new to old
s	by size, small to large
-s	by size, large to small
g	directories first
-g	directories last

For example, to sort the listing by size, from the
biggest to the smallest, type **DIR /O:-s**.

4. Press [←Enter].

DIR: Miscellaneous Switches You Can Use

Here's a listing of some of the more boring switches you can use with DIR, which we skipped earlier so you wouldn't fall asleep:

Switch	Purpose
/A	Shows files with all attributes, including hidden and system.
/A:*attrib*	Shows files with certain attributes:

	h	hidden
	-h	not hidden
	s	system
	-s	not system
	d	subdirectories (rather than files)
	-d	not subdirectories (actual files)
	a	archive files
	-a	not archive files
	r	read-only files
	-r	not read-only files

Switch	Purpose
/B	Shows the names and extensions separated by a period.
/L	Shows all names in lowercase.
/C	Displays the file's compression ratios if you're using DoubleSpace or DriveSpace.

DISKCOMP

DISKCOMP compares two diskettes and reports any differences in triplicate. (Not really—actually, it reports the differences on-screen, which you'll find handier, since you'll be looking at it.)

You can only compare diskettes of the same size (*size* size) and capacity (*storage* size) with DISKCOMP. You can't compare hard disks.

1. Type **DISKCOMP**.

2. Press [Spacebar].

3. Type the first disk's drive letter (followed by a colon, like this: *drive:*).

4. Press [Spacebar].

5. Type the second disk's drive letter (like this: *drive:*).

6. Press [↵Enter].

You'll be asked to remove the first diskette, and replace it with the second diskette if you're using a single drive for the comparison. If DISKCOMP finds any differences, it'll beep to let you know.

You can use the same drive for both disks. For example, **DISKCOMP A: A:**.

DISKCOPY

DISKCOPY copies an entire diskette to another diskette of the same size and capacity. Use this command to make copies of your program diskettes before your darling little Billy chews on them, leaving you with embarrassing prospect of calling the manufacturer to explain that you can't install your program because some of the installation diskettes were mistaken for Graham cracker squares by your two-year-old.

1. Type **DISKCOPY**.

2. Press [Spacebar].

3. Type the source drive letter (like this: *drive:*).

Reminder: the source and destination diskettes must be of the same dimension (*size* size) and capacity (*storage* size).

4. Press [Spacebar].

5. Type the destination drive letter (like this: *drive:*).

Try This!

For example, you could type **DISKCOPY A: A:** or **DISKCOPY A: B:**. You could also type **DISKCOPY ALL THESE DISKS WHILE I GO TAKE A COFFEE BREAK PLEASE**, but it wouldn't work.

6. Press [↵Enter]. You'll be asked to remove the first diskette, and replace it with the second diskette if you're using a single drive for the disk copy.

Just gotta know more about DISKCOPY? See *The Complete Idiot's Guide to DOS*, Chapter 17, "AUTOEXEC.BAT, CONFIG.SYS, and Other Secret Code Words."

DOS

The DOS command lets you load DOS into the high-memory area. Why would DOS want to go into high memory? Why, to get to the other side. Actually, it's to make room in conventional memory for more important things, namely your *programs*. This command works only in the CONFIG.SYS file; you can't use it at the DOS prompt. OK, so you can type "DOS" at the DOS prompt, but don't expect it to answer you.

See the section, "Hacking Away at Files With the DOS Editor" to learn how to insert this command into your CONFIG.SYS without losing your mind.

On a new line in your CONFIG.SYS file, *after* the commands DEVICE=C:\DOS\HIMEM.SYS and DEVICE=C:\DOS\EMM386.EXE, type this command:

```
DOS=HIGH,UMB
```

The `,UMB` part makes it possible for DOS to create upper memory blocks (UMBs) so you can load device drivers into high memory. Don't worry about what this means right now; just do it this way and you'll be fine.

For DOS=HIGH to work, you must also have this command in your CONFIG.SYS (*above* the DOS=HIGH,UMB line):

```
DEVICE=C:\DOS\HIMEM.SYS
```

For the ,UMB part to work, make sure this command is *above* the DOS=HIGH,UMB command as well (but *below* the HIMEM.SYS line. Stop me if this is getting confusing.):

```
DEVICE=C:\EMM386.EXE
```

For more info on the DOS command, see *The Complete Idiot's Guide to DOS*, Chapter 17, "AUTOEXEC.BAT, CONFIG.SYS, and Other Secret Code Words."

DOSKEY

DOSKEY is a great command for lousy typists, because it stores DOS commands as you enter them, and allows you to recall and reuse them (without retyping them). You can even recall and edit them (a good feature for really, *really* lousy typists who need a couple of tries to get a DOS command typed in correctly.)

DOSKEY: Installing DOSKEY

To install DOSKEY so it remembers your commands:

1. Type **DOSKEY**.

2. Press ⏎Enter.

DOSKEY: Recalling Commands

To use DOSKEY to recall a previously typed DOS command:

1. Press ↑ until the desired previous command appears.

2. Edit the command by pressing ← or → and retyping.

3. Press ⏎Enter to execute the command.

To show all the commands in DOSKEY's memory, press F7. To select a DOS command from the list as your next date, press F9 then type the number of the command you want to use. The command you selected will squeal in delight and appear at the prompt. Press ⏎Enter to execute the command.

To erase the previous commands from DOSKEY's memory, press Alt + F7.

DOSSHELL

The DOS Shell is a graphical interface that keeps you safe and warm, miles away from the cold, black-and-white world of the DOS prompt. Inside the Shell, you can perform the same commands that you could outside the Shell at the nasty old DOS prompt, but with greater ease (and somewhat better understanding).

The DOS Shell is not included with DOS 6.2, but you may have it already, if your PC used an older version of DOS at one time. If the DOS Shell has gone AWOL, you can order a copy of the Shell from Microsoft Support.

To start the DOS Shell:

1. Type **DOSSHELL**.

2. Press (↵Enter).

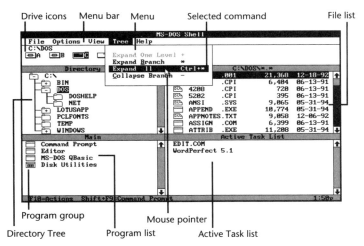

Now that you've got the thing up and running, check out the section, "Playing the DOS Shell Game" at the back of this book for details on what you can do. You can also check out *The Complete Idiot's Guide to DOS*, Chapter 8, "Worth the Price of Admission—The DOS Shell" for a kind and gentle introduction, if you happen to have it handy.

DRVSPACE

Where there was one, now there are two. DriveSpace (the younger sister of DoubleSpace) effectively doubles the amount of free space on your hard disk, allowing you to put more games and other things on it. For example, if you have a mere 25MB of free space, you'll end up with about 50MB. How this works doesn't matter, since it's pretty much invisible to you, the user. You use your DriveSpaced drive the same way as you did before.

DoubleSpace came with DOS 6.0 and 6.2. In DOS 6.22 it was replaced by DriveSpace, which works pretty much the same way. (What's different is the parts underneath that do the actual compression.) If you have DoubleSpace, use the steps here without fear—just remember to type **DBLSPACE** instead of DRVSPACE to start the program.

If you currently use another disk-compression program such as Stacker, don't worry—your Microsoft documentation just happens to be full of information about converting to DriveSpace. (Imagine that.) For that matter, you can easily convert your DoubleSpaced drive to DriveSpace too—see "Converting a DoubleSpaced Drive to DriveSpace" in this section.

To begin enjoying the comforts of DriveSpace in your own home or workplace, the first thing you should do is compress your hard disk. So I've conveniently placed the section, "Compressing a Drive With DriveSpace" right here where you can find it. After that, all the remaining commands in this section are alphabetized for your reading pleasure.

For more about DriveSpace than you might care to know, see *The Complete Idiot's Guide to DOS*, Chapter 19, "Double Your Pleasure, Double Your Fun, Double Your Disk."

DRVSPACE: Compressing a Drive with DriveSpace

If you've never run DriveSpace before, the first thing you must do is let it convert your ordinary hard disk into a super-cool-compressed hard disk. Be the first one on your block with enough room to install three, count 'em three, complete Windows programs.

It takes roughly one minute per megabyte of data to compress your hard disk, so you might want to start the DoubleSpace or DriveSpace setup program at the end of the day and run it overnight. Or you can just excuse yourself and go home early for the day. (Darn, I'm really sorry boss, but I'm just gonna have to go home early.)

1. Exit all programs, including the DOS Shell and Windows.

2. Type **DRVSPACE** (or **DBLSPACE**).

3. Press ⏎Enter].

4. Welcome to DriveSpace. Press ⏎Enter to move along.

5. Click on **Express**, then press ⏎Enter.

6. **(Optional)** If you want to change the default letter for the uncompressed drive, click on that option, and type a new drive letter followed by a colon (like this: *drive:*).

7. Press C to Continue or F3 to chicken out.

8. After the disk compression is finished, a summary will display, showing information on the compressed drive. Press ⏎Enter and your system will restart with the compressed drive active and ready to play.

DRVSPACE (or DBLSPACE) creates a new drive letter (usually H:) for the remaining uncompressed space, and the compressed drive becomes your main (C:) hard disk. So to access your shiny new compressed drive, type **C:** and press ⏎Enter.

When you start your computer from now on, DriveSpace will do its thing. You just go on and do yours. There are no changes necessary to the way you do anything. Drive C: is still drive C:. It just has more room, that's all.

DRVSPACE: Changing the Size of a Compressed Drive

If your compressed drive is starting to feel a little tight around its middle, you can increase the size of your compressed drive—that is, provided you have enough uncompressed area to expand into.

There is a fixed amount of disk space available, and it's split between your compressed drive (C:) and your uncompressed drive (H:). Changing the size of C: will cause a corresponding change in H:'s size. You might want to give your uncompressed portion more space, for example, if you want to install a large program there. (Why you'd want to install a program on an uncompressed drive is beyond me, unless the poor thing is so stupid it won't work right any other way, but I haven't run into one yet that had a problem with DriveSpace.)

1. Exit all programs, including the DOS Shell.
2. Type **DRVSPACE** (or **DBLSPACE**) and press ⏎Enter.
3. Click on **Drive**.
4. Click on **Change Size**.
5. Enter the amount of space you want to leave in the uncompressed portion of your drive.

Enter the amount of space you want to
leave on your uncompressed drive

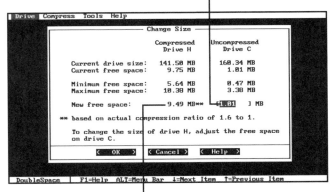

The remainder is given to the compressed drive

In step 5, the leftover space is then assigned to the compressed drive. (Kinda backwards, I know.)

6. Click on **OK**.

7. This process takes awhile, so have a seat. When it's done, exit the maintenance program by clicking on **Drive** and clicking on **Exit**.

DRVSPACE: Checking a Compressed Disk

If you want to check your compressed drive and remove any junk DOS sometimes leaves around during its normal file maintenance process (such a slob!), you run SCANDISK just like you would on any other drive. Check out the SCANDISK command coming up later in the command-reference section of the book.

DRVSPACE: Compressing a Diskette

Once you've compressed your hard disk with DoubleSpace or DriveSpace, you don't have to stop there. You can use it to compress diskettes and improve their storage capacities. (This is done without pain or heavy objects.) After a diskette has been compressed, it'll hold almost twice as much data as before. I don't want to throw you into a compression depression, but there is one drawback to using compressed diskettes: you can use a compressed diskette only on a PC that is running DoubleSpace or DriveSpace.

1. Exit all programs, including the DOS Shell.

2. Insert the diskette in its drive, then type **DRVSPACE** (or **DBLSPACE**) and press ⏎Enter.

3. Click on **Compress**.

4. Click on **Existing Drive**.

5. If necessary, change the drive to compress. Press ⏎Enter.

6. After the disk is compressed, return to DOS by clicking on **Drive**, then clicking on **Exit**.

Now that the diskette has been compressed, use the diskette as you would any other: copy and delete files to your heart's content.

DRVSPACE: Converting a DoubleSpaced Drive to DriveSpace

If you've just upgraded to DOS 6.22, and your hard disk is DoubleSpaced, you can leave it as is, or you can convert it to DriveSpace (which I recommend, since DriveSpace is newer and contains 25% less fat). The conversion process is pretty painless, as you'll soon see, and it doesn't take nearly as long as it did to DoubleSpace the hard disk originally.

By the way, if you used the MS-DOS Upgrade diskettes (instead of the MS-DOS Step Up diskettes) to upgrade your system to DOS 6.22, then you don't have this conversion program. No foolin'. Take two steps back, then call Microsoft Support and in your nicest I-guess-you-don't-really-want-anyone-to-convert-to-DriveSpace-since-you-didn't-include-the-darn-diskette voice, calmly ask them to "Get that darn diskette out here ASAP." Then continue with the steps shown here to convert your DoubleSpace drive to DriveSpace.

If your drive was only partly converted to DriveSpace because of problems, type **DBLSPACE** from the C> prompt, click on **Tools**, then click on **Convert Doublespace**.

Before you start, play it safe: do a backup first (see the MSBACKUP command). If something goes wrong, you can use it to restore your original hard disk. I didn't run into any problems, but doing a backup before a complex procedure like this one is always a good idea.

Also, before you start, check your hard disk for "bytes free" by typing **DIR** and pressing ⏎Enter. You're gonna need around .6MB free (about 629,146 bytes) on the non-compressed drive (it's probably drive H:), and some free room to work on the compressed drive (drive C:). About two to four megabytes (2 million to 4 million bytes) should be adequate.

1. Exit all programs, including the DOS Shell.

2. Type **DRVSPACE** and press ⏎Enter.

3. You'll see a message warning you to do a backup. Since you already have, press ⏎Enter to continue.

4. Wait for DRVSPACE to check your disk with ScanDisk and then convert the drive.

DRVSPACE runs ScanDisk to check your disk first. Then it begins the conversion process. You can press F3 to quit at anytime, although I wouldn't do it. If you do run into problems and DriveSpace can't convert the entire drive, you won't be stuck because your PC will still work. But you should remedy the situation as soon as you can, and run DRVSPACE again to convert the rest of the drive.

5. When you see the message that DriveSpace is done, press ⏎Enter to restart your system with a DriveSpace drive. That's it. Congratulations—it's a DriveSpaced drive.

DRVSPACE: Defragmenting a Compressed Drive

DOS will never make Housekeeper of the Year. It's downright sloppy when it comes to keeping files organized on your hard disk. To get the lowdown on what actually happens and why defragging is generally a good thing to do, turn back to the DEFRAG command in this section. Before you do, however, keep in mind that defragging a *compressed* drive really doesn't do much at all, because a compressed drive stores files in a different way. (A better explanation would be pretty technical, so let's just leave it at that.) Defragmenting a compressed disk might free up a little bit of space, but that's about it.

If you still want to defrag your compressed drive, here's how:

1. Exit all programs, including the DOS Shell.

2. Type **DRVSPACE** (or **DBLSPACE**) and press ⏎Enter.

3. Click on the drive you wish to defragment.

4. Click on **Tools**.

5. Click on **Defragment**.

6. You'll see a message asking you if you really want to do this. Click on **Yes** to continue, then go on to step 7. If you've changed your mind, press (Esc) then go on to step 8.

7. When DEFRAG is done, click on **Drive**.

8. Click on **Exit**.

DRVSPACE: Rebooting Without Running DRVSPACE

If your hard disk is "on vacation" (it isn't working), you may want to bypass the DriveSpace startup procedure. (After taking about two dozen aspirin and calling in the cavalry, of course.)

Take note, techno-nerd wannabes: This emergency procedure should not be done unless there's a real big problem! Because if you don't allow DriveSpace to start, you won't be able to access any of the files on the drivespaced drive. Of course, if your hard disk isn't working anyway, then it doesn't matter.

To prevent DriveSpace from starting by bypassing the AUTOEXEC.BAT and CONFIG.SYS files:

1. Reboot your computer by pressing
   Ctrl + Alt + Caps Lock.

2. When you see the words **Starting DOS**, press
   Ctrl + F5.

To prevent DriveSpace from starting by selectively bypassing certain commands in the AUTOEXEC.BAT and CONFIG.SYS files:

1. Reboot your computer by pressing
   Ctrl + Alt + Caps Lock.

2. When you see the words **Starting DOS**, press
   Ctrl + F8.

3. Select lines within your AUTOEXEC.BAT and CONFIG.SYS files by pressing Y for those you want executed, or N for those you don't.

DRVSPACE: Uncompressing a Compressed Drive

Uncompressing a drive takes it back to where it was before you DriveSpaced (or DoubleSpaced) it. There's usually no reason to uncompress a drive, but so many people complained so bitterly that they couldn't do it with DOS 6.0 that Microsoft added the feature in DOS 6.2. (Yes, giant software companies really do listen, and occasionally include features that make no sense, just because the public thought they wanted them.) Good news if you decide you must do this: Uncompressing a compressed drive is easy. Bad news: Making room for the contents of the compressed drive may not be.

Keep in mind that you can't uncompress a drive with the DOS 6.0 version of DoubleSpace. At least not easily. True tech-head nerds can do it, but not without losing the entire contents of the drive. To uncompress a drive following these instructions and ignoring the techno-nerd route, you need the DOS 6.2 version of DoubleSpace.

It'll take about the same amount of time to uncompress a drive as it took to compress it (about 1MB a minute), so you might want to wait and start this process at the end of the day, so it can run overnight. Otherwise, you just might have to skip out of work early and go to the park because you won't be able to use your computer for awhile. Darn the luck.

1. Exit all programs, including the DOS Shell.

2. Type **DRVSPACE** and press ⏎Enter).

3. Click on **Tools**.

4. Click on **Uncompress**.

5. Follow the additional instructions on-screen. When it's done, your drive will be uncompressed.

ECHO

ECHO makes the computer repeat everything you say. (Just kidding.) Actually, ECHO controls what appears on-screen when a batch file such as the AUTOEXEC.BAT file is running. You can use this command only in a batch file, and not at the DOS prompt, so don't try it unless you're really bored.

To learn how to edit your AUTOEXEC.BAT, bring along your paring knife and check out the section, "Hacking Away at Files With the DOS Editor."

For more info on the ECHO command, see *The Complete Idiot's Guide to DOS*, Chapter 17, "AUTOEXEC.BAT, CONFIG.SYS, and Other Secret Code Words."

ECHO: Turning ECHO Off

On the first line in a batch file (such as AUTOEXEC.BAT), type this command. It turns ECHO off, so DOS commands will not display as your batch file is doing its thing. This makes for prettier (and more professional looking) batch files.

Type **@ECHO OFF**.

As silly as it may seem, typing @ in front of the ECHO command keeps the words "ECHO OFF" from appearing on-screen when this command is executed.

You can turn ECHO back on later in a batch file by typing ECHO ON. ECHO OFF does not prevent messages from ECHO itself (details coming up) from being displayed.

ECHO: Using ECHO to Display a Message

In a batch file (such as AUTOEXEC.BAT), this command enables you to display silly (or serious) messages on-screen. For best results, make sure that ECHO is off, by including the command given earlier as the first line in your batch file.

1. Type **ECHO**.

2. Press [Spacebar].

3. Type the message you want to display.

For example, you could use the command **ECHO Welcome to the wonderful world of PCs** to display your message on-screen at that point in the batch file.

If you want a blank line to appear on the screen, type ECHO followed by a period (as in **ECHO.**) instead of typing a message. This allows you to place your message in the middle of the screen where your sleeping user might see it when he or she wakes up.

This inserts a few blank lines on-screen.

```
  File  Edit  Search  Options                                    Help
                            SILLY.BAT
 @ECHO OFF                                   This turns echoing of
 CLS         This clears your screen.        commands off.
 ECHO.
 ECHO.
 ECHO   This message is brought to you by ECHO, which repeats anything
 ECHO   you tell it, because it doesn't know any better. After all,
 ECHO   it's only a DOS command.
 ECHO.
 ECHO.
 ECHO   Using CLS to clear the screen, followed by a bunch of ECHO. commands
 ECHO   causes your message to appear in the middle of the screen, instead of
 ECHO   whereever DOS feels like displaying it this time.
 ECHO.
 ECHO.
 ECHO   ECHO. is also handy for inserting blank lines in your message, which
 ECHO   breaks it up and makes it easier for the user to read. Whether they
 ECHO   understand the message at all is any one's guess.
 ECHO.
 ECHO   End your batch file with a final ECHO. to separate your last
 ECHO   message from the dumb DOS prompt.
 ECHO.
 MS-DOS Editor  <F1=Help> Press ALT to activate menus              N 00001:001
```

This ECHO command displays a message on-screen.

EDIT

EDIT starts Edit, the Cinemascope text editor. You can use EDIT to make changes to CONFIG.SYS, AUTOEXEC.BAT, and any other text file your little heart desires to tear up.

1. Type **EDIT**.

2. **(Optional)** Press ⬚ Spacebar ⬚ and type the name of the file you want to edit.

3. Press ⬚ ↵Enter ⬚.

For example, type **EDIT BIGMESS.TXT**.

You can see what the EDIT screen looks like by checking out the figure under ECHO (turn back a page or so). For more information about EDIT, see the intriguing section entitled, "Hacking Away at Files With the DOS Editor" at the back of this book. Be sure to bring your scissors.

If you've got a copy of *The Complete Idiot's Guide to DOS* and you're really into this EDIT thing, check out Chapter 16, "Who, Me? Edit My Startup Files?" for more info.

EMM386.EXE

This command is used by DOS to help it reach an area of memory called upper memory. When DOS was invented, 640K of RAM (the area now called *conventional memory*) was considered an enormous amount—more than anyone would ever need. As a consequence of this pathetic oversight, DOS needs help to use the areas of memory which were added later, such as upper memory. EMM386.EXE is a command that provides that stepping stone to upper memory. HIMEM.SYS, another popular command, provides access to extended memory (another of those Johnny-come-lately memory areas).

EMM386 is a clever fellow who not only provides access to upper memory, but converts some extended memory into expanded memory at a nominal charge. For a really deep look into memory, see "More Than You'll Want to Know About Configuring Your PC," later in this book.

> The EMM386.EXE command is placed in your CONFIG.SYS. See "Hacking Away at Files With the DOS Editor" section later in this book to learn the satisfying art of editing the CONFIG.SYS and other text files.

Type **one** of these commands on a new line right *after* the DEVICE=C:\DOS\HIMEM.SYS line of your CONFIG.SYS file, and *before* DOS=HIGH,UMB, or any DEVICEHIGH line.

For the scoop on memory and its torrid romance with the EMM386 command, see *The Complete Idiot's Guide to DOS*, Chapter 20, "Pump Up the RAM!"

EMM386: Simulating Expanded Memory

To use EMM386.EXE to simulate expanded memory, add the following to your CONFIG.SYS file:

1. Type `DEVICE=C:\DOS\EMM386.EXE`.
2. Press [Spacebar].
3. Type the amount (in kilobytes) of expanded memory you want.

> For example, to simulate 1,024KB (1 MB) of expanded memory, type `DEVICE=EMM386.EXE 1024`. If you don't specify any particular amount, then EMM386 makes a pig of itself and converts all available extended memory to expanded memory.

4. **(Optional)** To enable the use of the upper memory area as well, press ⌷ Spacebar ⌷ and type **RAM**.

Step four is necessary if you want access to upper memory as well as expanded memory (which, believe me, you do). But you'll have to have the additional command **DOS=HIGH,UMB** in your CONFIG.SYS to make it all work.

Check your program manuals and other paraphernalia to see if you need expanded memory to run your applications. For example, Windows (and Windows programs) cannot use expanded memory, so be sure you need the amount you allocate.

EMM386: Providing Extended Memory Only

To use EMM386.EXE to provide access to extended memory (no expanded memory at all), and to enable the use of the upper memory area, add the following to your CONFIG.SYS file. (Hint: This is a good command to include in your CONFIG.SYS if you're running Windows.)

1. Type **DEVICE=EMM386.EXE**.

2. Press ⌷ Spacebar ⌷.

3. Type **NOEMS**.

EXIT

Some programs (Windows being a very famous example) allow you to sneak out to DOS to perform some command, then sneak back to the main program, without having to really exit the main program at all. They do that by providing you with something called a *temporary DOS prompt*, otherwise known as a *shell*, thank you very much. (However, a temporary DOS prompt—a shell—is not like the DOS Shell with a capital "S" covered later in this book. I know it's confusing, but what do you expect? It's DOS.) Anyway, the ways you access a temporary DOS prompt within a program vary, but the way you return to your program usually does not: you return via the EXIT command.

Why would you want to use a temporary DOS prompt? Well, suppose you were working madly away in your spreadsheet program, and you wanted to save an important file onto a diskette, but you wanted to delete whatever was already on the diskette first. You'd issue the command in the program to access the temporary DOS prompt, then you'd type the DEL A:*.* command to delete the files on the diskette. After station identification, you'd type the EXIT command to return to your regularly scheduled program.

1. Access the temporary DOS prompt from within your program.

To find the temporary DOS prompt, look for commands like "Command Prompt," or "DOS Commands," or "Shell," or some such on one of the menus. If you want to use the temporary DOS prompt from within Windows 3.x, simply double-click on the **Main** program group to open it, then select (double-click on) the {MS-DOS Prompt} icon.

2. Type your DOS command as usual.

3. To return to your program, type **EXIT** and press ⏎Enter.

If you just hate to leave (exit) EXIT, see *The Complete Idiot's Guide to DOS*, Chapter 24, "Using DOS From Within Other Programs" for more info.

EXPAND

Use the EXPAND command to copy files from the MS-DOS 6.2 Setup diskettes onto your hard disk if you've accidentally deleted one or more of the DOS files. This command expands the skinny, unusable versions of these DOS files into bigger, totally usable versions.

To locate the setup diskette that contains the file you want to expand, insert one of the setup diskettes into drive A, type **DIR A: /P**, and press ⏎Enter. The files have the same names as they would when expanded, except their last character is an underscore (_).

1. Type **EXPAND**.

2. Press [Spacebar].

3. Type **A:**.

4. Type the name of the file to expand (like this: *filename.EX_*).

For example, to expand and copy the SORT file, type **A:\SORT.EX_**.

5. Press [Spacebar].

6. Type **C:\DOS**.

7. Type the real name of the DOS file (like this: *filename.EXE*).

For example, type **C:\DOS\SORT.EXE**.

8. Press ⏎Enter.

FASTHELP

FASTHELP gets Uncle Billy out of trouble fast, by providing a quick listing of parameters for a particular command. If you like this command, why not try the home version? (Now with expanded instructions and examples of each command. It's fun for the whole family.) See HELP.

1. Type **FASTHELP**.

2. Press [Spacebar].

3. Type the command for which you want help.

For example, to get help with the DIR command, type **FASTHELP DIR**.

```
C:\>fasthelp cd
Displays the name of or changes the current directory.

CHDIR [drive:][path]
CHDIR[..]
CD [drive:][path]
CD[..]

    ..   Specifies that you want to change to the parent directory.

Type CD drive: to display the current directory in the specified drive.
Type CD without parameters to display the current drive and directory.

C:\>
```

Another way to get the same results as FASTHELP is to take the shortcut. Just type the command, then /? (for example, **DIR /?**).

Want more help with Help? Check out *The Complete Idiot's Guide to DOS*, Chapter 9, "That's My Version and I'm Sticking to It."

FASTOPEN

FASTOPEN is slow, fat, and supposedly makes your hard disk faster by keeping frequently used files in memory where your PC can grab them quickly. FASTOPEN does this by creating a *disk cache* (pronounced "cash") to store all those frequently used files. To create this cache, however, FASTOPEN gobbles up regular memory your programs could use instead. So is there a benefit in using FASTOPEN? I don't know because I use SMARTDRV, since it also creates a cache, but it's a lot smarter about doing it.

As if you needed another reason to skip this section altogether, here it is: *DO NOT use FASTOPEN with Windows.* Use SMARTDRV instead. Also, from the I-warned-ya department: don't run a defragmentation program (such as DEFRAG) while FASTOPEN.EXE is loaded. Your data will get more scrambled than a dozen Humpty Dumptys. Also, don't use FASTOPEN to track files on a network drive. Big no-no.

If (for some crazy death-wish reason) you still want to run FASTOPEN, here's what you do. On a blank line within your CONFIG.SYS, type this:

1. Type: **INSTALL=**.

2. Type **C:\DOS\FASTOPEN.EXE**.

3. Press ⬚ Spacebar ⬚.

4. Type the drive you want to track (for example, **C:**).

5. Type an equals sign (=).

6. Type the maximum number of entries to be tracked (between 10 and 999).

For example, **INSTALL=C:\DOS\FASTOPEN.EXE C:=100**.

You can add the /X switch after the command to create the cache in expanded memory, instead of gobbling up regular (conventional) memory to create it. But if you're going to do this, of course, expanded memory must be available—like, duh. See EMM386.EXE for help.

FC

FC performs a primitive comparision of two files, and lets you know if they are the same. By primitive, I mean the silly utility actually displays each line that's different, instead of just simply saying, "They aren't the same. Try again." You can compare ASCII files (files which contain just text, and no formatting like bold, underline, etc.) or binary files (the other kind).

1. Type **FC**.

2. Press [Spacebar].

3. Type the location of the first file (like this: ***drive:\directory***).

4. Type the name of the first file (like this: ***filename.ext***).

5. Press [Spacebar].

6. Type the location of the second file.

7. Type the name of the second file.

8. **(Optional)** If you're comparing two binary files, press [Spacebar] and type **/B**.

9. **(Optional)** If you're comparing two ASCII files, press [Spacebar] and type **/A**.

Steps 8 and 9 are mutually exclusive; that is, you would use one or the other, never both. But then, you knew that already, right?

10. Press [↵Enter].

FDISK

FDISK was there at the birth of your hard disk, taking home movies and preparing it for use. Using it again will cause your hard disk to be "reborn," with all its contents sent to data heaven. Not recommended unless your hard disk is completely trashed, and you don't expect to recover any of the data on it anyway. Even then, this command is not for the faint of heart.

CAUTION! Some hard disks may not have been prepared for use with FDISK, but with some third-party program such as Speedstor, Everex, Disk Manager, or Priam. If you use FDISK on them, you'll wish you hadn't. To see whether one of these critters is involved, look for the presence of a DEVICE command which uses one of these files in your CONFIG.SYS: DMDRVVR.BIN, SSTOR.SYS, HARDRIVE.SYS, or EVDSK.SYS. If it exists, use the third-party program to *repartition* (create usable sections on) your hard disk.

1. Type **FDISK**.

2. Press ⏎Enter.

3. Follow the on-screen instructions.

You can get your feet wet (without getting too soaked) by simply checking out the status of your hard disk, and not repartitioning. Type **FDISK /STATUS** and press ⏎Enter.

FILES

Increases the number of files a program can open at one time from a measly 8 (the default) to whatever you specify (up to 255). Most programs that you purchase will specify a recommended FILES setting; check out the documentation or otherwise useless paraphernalia for all the programs you own, and set the FILES setting to the highest number asked for.

Tip

This command is used in the CONFIG.SYS file, so don't try typing it at the DOS prompt. For information about editing the CONFIG.SYS file, see the ever-exciting "Hacking Away at Files With the DOS Editor" section later in this book.

On a new line in the CONFIG.SYS file:

1. Type **FILES**=.

2. Type the desired number.

A common number to use is 30; this can be increased if a program error message tells you "Not Enough File Handles—Give Me More."

The super secret confidential file on FILES can be found in *The Complete Idiot's Guide to DOS*, Chapter 17, "AUTOEXEC.BAT, CONFIG.SYS, and Other Secret Code Words."

FIND

FIND determines whether the file or files you specify contain a specific text string. Sorry, but FIND cannot be used to locate other items (such as your keys, your wallet, or the jerk in MIS who set up your PC so you hear the sound of a toilet flushing every time you delete a file).

Try This!

For example, you can use FIND to locate the file which contains the missing sales report that your boss has been screaming for ever since he came in this morning. Then you could take two aspirin and move on to the next crisis.

1. Type **FIND**.

2. Press [Spacebar].

3. Type a text string to search for, in quotation marks (like this: **"text"**).

4. Press [Spacebar].

5. Type the location of the file to search (like this: **drive:\directory**).

6. Type the filename (like this: **filename.ext**).

For example, type: **FIND "you may have already won" C:\JUNK\BOGUSMIL.LTR**.

7. **(Optional)** Type a switch from the handsome collection below:

Switch	Purpose
/V	Shows all lines that don't contain the string.
/C	Counts the occurrences of the string but doesn't display them.
/N	Displays the line number before each displayed line.
/I	Ignores case when searching for the text string (uppercase or lowercase).

8. Press [↵Enter].

You can search through multiple files by using the FOR command with the FIND. This gets a bit tricky, so here's an example:

```
FOR %f IN (*.DOC) DO FIND "Where is it" %f
```

This command searches the current directory for all the DOC files, then looks in each of 'em to see if they contain the haunting words, "Where is it." If you use this command in a batch file, it should look like this instead:

```
FOR %%f IN (*.DOC) DO FIND "Where is it" %%f
```

You're probably scratching your head right now, so if you want some relief, check out the FOR command for more information.

FOR

Tired of repeating yourself? Use this command in a batch file or at the DOS prompt to repeat a DOS command several times on a series of files.

In a batch file, or at a DOS prompt, type this command:

1. Type **FOR**.

2. Press [Spacebar].

3. Type two percent signs, then some letter (like this: **%%letter**).

If you're using the FOR command at the DOS prompt (rather than in a batch file like AUTOEXEC.BAT), take it easy on the percent signs (%). Just one will do, as in: **FOR %a**.

4. Press [Spacebar] and type **IN**.

5. Press [Spacebar].

6. Type (in parentheses and separated by spaces) the names of all the files on which you want to perform the DOS command, like this:
   (filename filename)

Try This!

For example, type: **FOR %%a (ONE.DOC TWO.DOC THREE.DOC FOUR.DOC)**. Specify as many files as you like; just be sure to press [Spacebar] to separate each one. You can also use wildcards and directories to specify your files (again, separate them with a space): **FOR %%a (C:\JUNK*.BAD C:\TEMP*.*)**

7. Press [Spacebar] and type **DO**.

8. Press [Spacebar].

9. Type your command, including the %%letter where the filename would normally go, like this: *command %%letter*.

Try This!

Here's a complete example of the whole thing:

    FOR %%a IN (C:\JUNK*.BAD C:\JUNK*.DUM
    C:\PILE*.*) DO DEL %%a

What's this command do, oh wise one? Well, it searches the C:\JUNK directory for .BAD and .DUM files, then deletes them one at a time.

FORMAT

FORMAT prepares a diskette for use by ordinary human beings like yourself, by annihilating any existing files and directories stored there and setting up a nice area for organizing files. Imagine printing lines on a piece of notebook paper so the person who uses it will be able to write legibly, and you'll get an idea of what formatting does. Rest your weary head, 'cause you only need to do this command once in a diskette's life. If you're really smart, you can buy the critters already formatted and save yourself some time.

But if you insist, you can format a diskette as many times as you like, especially if you're trying to appear busy until it's time to go home. But it's not necessary— once a diskette is formatted, it's permanently formatted. Formatting the diskette again won't do anything except erase the diskette's contents (but if that's all you want to do, the DEL command is much faster).

If you goof and format a diskette your boss needs desperately, it might not mean your job; see the UNFORMAT command.

FORMAT: Formatting a Plain Old Diskette

1. Type **FORMAT**.

2. Press [Spacebar].

3. Insert the diskette into the drive, and type the drive letter (like this: *drive:*).

For example, type **FORMAT A:**.

4. **(Optional)** To format the diskette more quickly, press [Spacebar] and type /**U**.

Using /U causes an *unconditional* format, which means that FORMAT doesn't take the time to save the stuff it might need later if you decide, "Oops. Formatted the wrong diskette!" So be careful—don't use /U on a diskette you might want to unformat someday.

5. **(Optional)** To retest parts of the diskette that were previously marked as bad or unusable, press [Spacebar] and type /**C**.

6. Press ⏎Enter.

7. When asked to confirm, press ⏎Enter.

8. When asked, type a `volume label` if you want.

For example, in step 8 type **BOGUS SALES**. You're
limited to 11 characters here (and a space counts as
one of them), so you can't get too creative. I know;
I've tried.

9. If you want to format another diskette, press Y.
   Otherwise, press N.

This tells you how much room is on the
diskette, and if there are any bad spots.

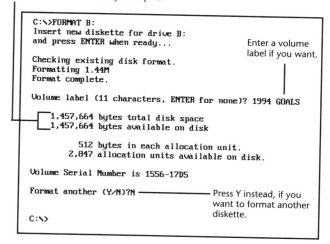

```
C:\>FORMAT B:
Insert new diskette for drive B:
and press ENTER when ready...          Enter a volume
                                       label if you want.
Checking existing disk format.
Formatting 1.44M
Format complete.

Volume label (11 characters, ENTER for none)? 1994 GOALS

  ┌─1,457,664 bytes total disk space
  └─1,457,664 bytes available on disk

        512 bytes in each allocation unit.
      2,847 allocation units available on disk.

Volume Serial Number is 1556-17D5

Format another (Y/N)?N ──────────── Press Y instead, if you
                                    want to format another
C:\>                                diskette.
```

FORMAT: Formatting a Double-Density Diskette in a High-Density Drive

Every diskette comes in one of two densities: *high-density*
or *double-density*. The *density* of a diskette refers to how
closely data can be packed onto the disk. A diskette

that's more dense than another diskette holds more data. Imagine one phonograph record with 100 grooves (for members of Generation X: a *record* was a black plastic pizza-like disk on which music was recorded, back in the days when music was worth making a record of), and a second record (the same size) with 200 grooves. On the latter, the grooves are closer together, so more music fits on the record. With diskettes, a high-density diskette holds about twice as much data as the same size double-density diskette.

You should purchase diskettes which match the density of your PC's diskette drive. So if your PC has a high-density drive, buy high-density diskettes for it. But in case you decide to forgo my infinite wisdom and buy double-density diskettes because they're cheaper, you can still format them this way: (Just don't put anything too important on those diskettes once they're formatted. OK? Because they're not too reliable when used this way.)

1. Type **FORMAT**.

2. Press ⬚ Spacebar ⬚.

3. Insert the diskette into the drive and type the drive letter (like this: *drive:*).

4. Press ⬚ Spacebar ⬚ and type **/F:360** (for a 5.25-inch diskette) or **/F:720** (for a DD 3.5-inch diskette).

5. Press ⬚Enter⬚.

6. Follow steps 7 to 9 under "FORMAT: Formatting a Plain Old Diskette."

FORMAT: Performing a Quick Format

If a diskette has already been formatted once and you want to delete the files on it, you can use the DEL command, or take the long way around with this command:

1. Type **FORMAT**.

2. Press [Spacebar].

3. Insert the diskette into the drive, and type the drive letter (like this: ***drive:***).

4. Press [Spacebar] and type **/Q**.

5. Press [⏎Enter].

6. Now follow steps 7 to 9 under "FORMAT: Formatting a Plain Old Diskette."

FORMAT: Formatting a Bootable Diskette

This slight twist on the FORMAT command creates a diskette you can use to start up your computer, in case your hard disk is ever rendered unusable.

1. Type **FORMAT**.

2. Press [Spacebar].

3. Insert the diskette into the drive, and type the drive letter (like this: ***drive:***).

5. Press [Spacebar] and type: **/S**.

6. Press [⏎Enter].

7. Now follow steps 7 to 9 under "FORMAT: Formatting a Plain Old Diskette."

GOTO

The GOTO command allows you to send your batch file spinning in another direction. When a GOTO command is encountered in a batch file, DOS jumps over other commands, straight to the place in the batch file where it was told to go. Now that's an obedient batch file!

This command is usually used in conjunction with the IF command, so that if a particular condition is true, DOS will jump to some other part of the batch file. Also useful for jumping over commands to the end of a batch file.

See the section, "Hacking Away at Files With the DOS Editor," a fun-filled look at editing text and batch files. Can't wait.

On some line in your batch file:

1. Type **GOTO**.

2. Press [Spacebar].

3. Type the name of the place you want DOS to land when it jumps within the batch file.

GOTO: Marking Where to Go

At some later point in the batch file, insert a line: **:*LABEL*** which matches the label name you used in your GOTO command. For example, you might type this in your batch file:

```
GOTO WKLY
```

Then, later in the batch file, you could insert commands for a weekly backup. Precede them with this line:

```
:WKLY
(type the commands for a weekly backup here)
```

When DOS encounters the GOTO command, it looks for the :WKLY label, and jumps to the commands which follow it.

This causes the batch file to jump over the Weekly commands and to go to the label marked "END."

Test to see if the user typed "W" for weekly backup, then jump to "WEEKLY."

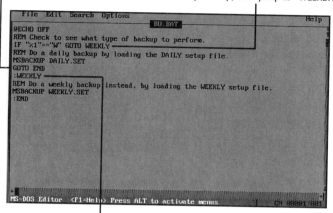

If the user typed a "W," the batch file jumps to this point.

HELP

HELP provides DOS help for the tired, poor, or down-trodden masses. Faster than a speeding bullet, DOS provides scads of help. (Whether you can actually make any sense of it is another matter.) This command provides more detail than using FASTHELP (described, not surprisingly, under "F" earlier in this section).

To start HELP:

1. Type **HELP**.

2. **(Optional)** Press ⸢ Spacebar ⸣ and type a command you need help with.

For example, type **HELP FORMAT** to get help with the FORMAT command.

3. Press ⏎Enter).

If you don't specify a command and you type just **HELP** by itself, you'll get the Table of Contents screen, from which you can select a command by simply clicking on it.

For more help with Help, see *The Complete Idiot's Guide to DOS*, Chapter 9, "That's My Version and I'm Sticking With It."

HELP: Navigating the DOS Help System Without a Map

Once inside the DOS Help system, you can move around at will. (Just be careful not to trip over the cables.) The syntax is fairly difficult to read, and why bother, since you have this book to translate it all for you? Here's how to move on to something useful:

Click here to view extra information.   Click here to view examples of the command.

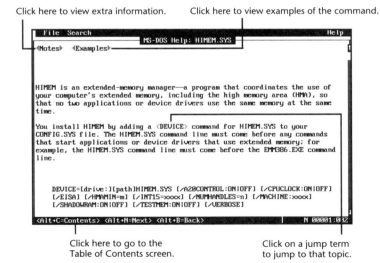

Click here to go to the
Table of Contents screen.

Click on a jump term
to jump to that topic.

To move here . . .	Do this . . .
To see the next screen	Press `PgDn`.
To go back to a previous screen	Press `PgUp`.
To jump to another section of Help	Click on a *jump term* (a word in angle brackets, such as <Tree>).
To view examples	Click on **Examples** at the top of the screen.
To view some interesting tidbits	Click on **Notes** at the top of the screen.
To go to the table of contents	Click on **Contents** at the bottom of the screen.

HELP: Exiting DOS Help

To exit the Help system:

1. Click on **File**.

2. Click on **Exit**.

HIMEM.SYS

This command is used by DOS to help it reach an area of memory called *extended memory*. EMM386.EXE is a pal which works together with HIMEM.SYS to create *expanded* memory out of extended memory and spare parts. Without going into the gory details, your PC's RAM is divided into different sections (such as extended memory), most of which came along after DOS was invented, so DOS needs help getting to these different areas of memory. With a ladder and the HIMEM.SYS command loaded in your CONFIG.SYS, DOS can reach extended memory. For a deeper look into memory, see "More Than You'll Want to Know About Configuring Your PC" later in this book.

This command is placed in your CONFIG.SYS. See the "Hacking Away at Files With the DOS Editor" section, later in this book, to learn the ancient but well-practiced art of editing the CONFIG.SYS and other text files.

In the **first** line of your CONFIG.SYS, type this line:

```
DEVICE=C:\DOS\HIMEM.SYS.
```

That's it! Pretty simple, huh?

For more memories, see *The Complete Idiot's Guide to DOS*, Chapter 20, "Pump Up the RAM!"

IF

Like Judge Wapner, the IF command presides over your batch file, weighing consequences and results. With the IF command, you can get your batch file to perform one thing if some condition is true, and something else if it's false.

You can reverse this whole process by using IF NOT instead: if the condition is false, the action is carried out. If the condition's true, it's not. Kinda like the logic the government uses to make decisions: If it's too messed up, don't fix it. If it's OK, mess it up.

To learn the Ginsu art of batch-file editing, see the section, "Hacking Away at Files With the DOS Editor" later in this book.

IF: Testing for the Existence of Files

Use this variation of the IF command to perform some action only if a file exists. Somewhere in a batch file:

1. Type **IF**.

2. **(Optional)** If you want to do the command only if the file *doesn't exist*, press [Spacebar] and type: **NOT.**

3. Press [Spacebar] and type **EXIST**.

4. Press [Spacebar].

4. **(Optional)** Type the location of the file (like this: *drive*:*directory*\\).

5. Type the name of the file.

6. Press [Spacebar] and type the command you want carried out.

Try This!

For example, type

```
IF NOT EXIST C:\SAFE.BAK COPY SAFE.BAT
SAFE.BAK
```

You can use a variety of commands, depending on your mood:

```
IF EXIST C:\SLOB.DOC GOTO OSCAR
```

or

```
IF NOT EXIST C:\MYFILES\IMPT.DOC ECHO Oh,
Oh!
```

IF: Checking For ERRORLEVEL Conditions

Some polite DOS commands (such as FORMAT, COPY, and CHOICE) produce ERRORLEVEL codes when they run. Generally, ERRORLEVEL=0 when the commands work, and other ERRORLEVELs when they don't. Check the DOS Help system for a listing of ERRORLEVELS that correspond to the command you want to test.

1. Type **IF**.

2. **(Optional)** If you want to do the command only if the error *doesn't exist*, press ⌷ Spacebar ⌷ and type **NOT**.

3. Press ⌷ Spacebar ⌷ and type **ERRORLEVEL**.

4. Press ⌷ Spacebar ⌷ and type the number you want to test for: *number*.

5. Press ⌷ Spacebar ⌷ and type the command you want carried out: *command*.

Try This!

For example, type:

```
IF NOT ERRORLEVEL 0 ECHO Big time problemo!
```

IF: Checking Startup Parameters

When you start a batch file, you can give it parameters in which to work, just like you do for your kids: "Now, kids, don't jump on the coffee table in months ending in R." In a batch file, the parameters might be the name of a file you want to copy, or a word which tells the batch file which variation to perform (such as a weekly backup instead of a daily backup). With this variation of the IF command, you can test what these parameters are equal to, and then take the appropriate action.

1. Type **IF**.

2. **(Optional)** If you want to do the command only if the two things *don't match*, press ⌷ Spacebar ⌷ and type **NOT**.

3. Press ⌷ Spacebar ⌷ and type, in quotation marks, a percent sign and then a number, like this: *"%number"*.

For example, suppose a user is performing a weekly backup with the batch file BU.BAT, and types

BU WKLY B:

%1 (the first parameter) is equal to WKLY and %2 (the second parameter for this batch file) is equal to B:. By the way, %0 is equal to BU, the name of the batch file.

4. Type: `=="string"`.

For example, to test to see whether the user wants a weekly backup performed, type this:

IF "%1"=="WKLY"

Note the quotation marks and the double equal signs. If you miss one of these, the command won't work.

5. Press [Spacebar] and type the command you want carried out.

For example, you can test to see which drive the user wants the batch file to use, and go to another part of the batch file if he wants to use B drive instead of the A drive:

IF "%2"=="B:" GOTO BDRIVE

INCLUDE

INCLUDE is one of the privileged batch file commands that help you create a menu system so you can make some choices about how your computer starts up. Specifically, INCLUDE allows you to include commands associated with one menu item within another menu item in your CONFIG.SYS.

Sorry, but you have to put this command in your CONFIG.SYS; you can't type it at a DOS prompt, unless you want DOS nerds around the world to laugh at you. To learn how to chop up your CONFIG.SYS, see the section, "Hacking Away at Files With the DOS Editor" later in this book.

Would you like to see a menu? Check out the commands: MENUCOLOR, MENUDEFAULT, MENUITEM, and SUBMENU, and the section, "More Than You'll Want to Know About Configuring Your PC."

On a line in your CONFIG.SYS:

1. Type **INCLUDE=**.

2. Type the name of the group of commands you want included in this group of commands if this menu item is chosen: *grouplabel*.

For example, suppose that earlier in the CONFIG.SYS, you'd identified a group of commands with the name BASIC_CONFIG, (by typing the label **[BASIC_CONFIG]** and then typing the commands you wanted for that group under the label). Now you want to include those commands with another group that configures your system for running games. Type your INCLUDE command under the group label for the game commands:

```
[GAMES_CONFIG]
INCLUDE=BASIC_CONFIG
```

When the user chooses Games from the menu, the commands under [BASIC_CONFIG] in the CONFIG.SYS will be executed, along with the commands under [GAMES_CONFIG].

INTERLNK

Creates a kind of "information super-sidewalk" between two PCs, such as a desktop PC and a portable. You can then transfer files between the two PCs, print files on your portable using the desktop's printer, and other neat things like that.

One PC (usually the desktop) is called the *Server* because it provides stuff like disk drives, a printer, etc., while the other PC (called the *Client*) just takes and takes and never visits, except once a year at Christmas. Once the Client is connected to the Server, you can print files using the Server's printer, run programs on the Server, copy files, etc.

The shopping list you need to make this possible:

➤ Both PCs need at least DOS 6.

➤ You need to connect the two PCs through a null modem cable, whatever that is. See your local dealer or PC guru for help.

To set it up, on the Client (laptop) PC, add this command to the CONFIG.SYS:

1. Type **DEVICE**=.

2. Type **C:\DOS\INTERLNK.EXE**.

Now, to get the magic to work, you need to connect the two PCs with the null modem cable, restart the laptop PC, and type the **INTERSVR** command on the Server (see the next command for help).

If you'd like to know more about what you're doing here (and why you're the one stuck doing it), see *The Complete Idiot's Guide to DOS*, Chapter 25, "It's a Portable PC World Out There!"

INTERSVR

INTERSVR provides the other half of the information super-sidewalk. This command is used on the Server PC to help it provide its services (the disk drives, printer, etc.) in a friendly manner, without fist fights.

INTERSVR differs from the INTERLNK command which is placed in the CONFIG.SYS of the Client PC; you can simply type this command at the DOS prompt. (What a relief!)

At the DOS prompt on the Server PC, type this command:

1. Type **CD\DOS** and press ⏎Enter).

2. Type **INTERSVR**.

Now you're in business! Go over to the Client PC, transfer files, run programs, print things, and basically have a ball. The Server PC will never know the difference. When the party's over, call a cab, then go over to the Server PC and press Alt) + F4).

The two PCs will part company, and you can once again use them separately.

LABEL

LABEL slaps an electronic label on a diskette, so the next time you're looking for the only copy of your 1994 sales report, you might actually find it in less than an hour. You can also slap a label on your hard disk, but I'm not sure why you'd want to do that, since it's not going anywhere, so the chances of your misplacing it are probably not very high.

As an added bonus, this electronic label is displayed whenever you type **DIR** to see the contents of that particular diskette or hard disk.

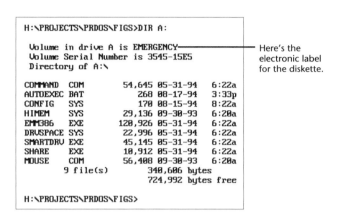

```
H:\PROJECTS\PRDOS\FIGS>DIR A:

 Volume in drive A is EMERGENCY
 Volume Serial Number is 3545-15E5
 Directory of A:\

COMMAND  COM      54,645 05-31-94   6:22a
AUTOEXEC BAT         268 08-17-94   3:33p
CONFIG   SYS         170 08-15-94   8:22a
HIMEM    SYS      29,136 09-30-93   6:20a
EMM386   EXE     120,926 05-31-94   6:22a
DRVSPACE SYS      22,996 05-31-94   6:22a
SMARTDRV EXE      45,145 05-31-94   6:22a
SHARE    EXE      10,912 05-31-94   6:22a
MOUSE    COM      56,400 09-30-93   6:20a
         9 file(s)        340,606 bytes
                         724,992 bytes free

H:\PROJECTS\PRDOS\FIGS>
```

Here's the electronic label for the diskette.

You can save yourself some time, and enter the darn label when you format the diskette in the first place. See the FORMAT command.

1. Type **LABEL**.

2. Press [Spacebar]

3. Type the letter of the drive you want to label (like this: *drive***:**).

4. Press [Spacebar] and type the label.

For example, type **LABEL A: PHONEY FIGS**.

4. Press [⏎Enter].

You can use up to 11 characters in your label, including spaces. Labels are always presented in uppercase, regardless of whether they went to Princeton or Harvard, or how they were entered. Just don't go crazy and try to use any of the following characters in a volume label:

> * ? / \ | . , ; : + = [ ] ( ) & ^ < > "

Haven't heard enough about the fascinating world of electronic labels? Well, check out *The Complete Idiot's Guide to DOS*, Chapter 6, "Diskette Disco".

LASTDRIVE

In the dark ages of early DOS versions, this command was used to specify the allowable drive letters for your PC. The default back then was the letter E, so if you had a network drive called N, you couldn't use it without this command. This was stupid, so the programmers at Microsoft changed it. Now DOS analyzes your PC automatically, and sets the value to whatever you need, plus one to grow on. For example, if your PC has drives A, B, and C, then LASTDRIVE is set automatically to D.

If you've compressed your hard disk (see DRVSPACE), your one physical hard disk now has a dual identity: drives C: and H:. (DriveSpace and DoubleSpace know this will freak DOS, so they insert LASTDRIVE=H in your CONFIG.SYS to make it OK. *Don't remove this command under penalty of law.*) Nowadays, unless you want to start carving *logical drives* out of your physical hard disk drive (an ancient and barbaric art), you won't need to use LASTDRIVE.

OK, if you insist on trying to use this command when you probably don't need to, remember that LASTDRIVE only works in the CONFIG.SYS file; so don't try typing it at the DOS prompt. For information about slicing and dicing your CONFIG.SYS file, see the section, "Hacking Away at Files With the DOS Editor" later in this book.

On a blank line in your CONFIG.SYS file, after all the important stuff you really need:

1. Type **LASTDRIVE**=.

2. Type a drive letter (A through Z) *drive*.

LOADFIX

LOADFIX fixes the problem that some old-fogey programs have with loading DOS into high memory. You see, moving DOS into high memory and out of regular conventional memory (with the DOS=HIGH command) gives programs more room to play around with. Some older programs totally freak at this arrangement, refusing to load into the area of conventional memory once held as the royal land of DOS. LOADFIX takes your silly program and places it in conventional memory, above 64K, which marks the edge of what was once sacred ground (the area where DOS would be if you hadn't loaded it into high memory).

If you didn't understand one word of this discussion, that's OK, because the only thing you need to know is this: use the LOADFIX command when you try to start a program and get the message, "Packed File Corrupt" instead.

1. Type **LOADFIX**.

2. Press ⌐ Spacebar ⌐.

3. Type the location of the program you want to load (like this: *drive*:*directory*\).

4. Type the name of the program.

LOADHIGH (LH)

LOADHIGH places TSRs on high shelves in memory, so they don't clutter up the place and get in the way of your regular programs. TSRs (terminate-and-stay-resident programs) are special utilities which load into memory and then "go to sleep" until they are "awakened" by some event or a magic kiss. (VSAFE, the DOS virus-detection program, is one such TSR. Loaded into memory through the AUTOEXEC.BAT, it lounges around until it detects a change to a file that might indicate a computer virus.) LOADHIGH takes these memory-resident critters and pushes them into upper memory, where they can snooze out of the way of regular programs.

If device drivers (such as the one which controls your mouse or your CD-ROM) are getting in your way too, throw them into upper memory along with your TSRs. See the DEVICEHIGH command for help.

You can type the LOADHIGH command (or use his nickname, LH, if you're a close and dear friend) at the DOS prompt, or add it to the AUTOEXEC.BAT to load your TSR each time you start your PC.

1. Type **LH**.

2. Press [Spacebar].

3. Type the location of the name of the TSR program you want to shove into upper memory, like this: ***drive*:*directory***.

4. Type the name of the TSR.

5. Press [↵Enter].

You can also include any parameters that you normally use with a program, LOADHIGH is not particular. For example, this command starts the mouse-driver program with the /Y parameter:

`LH C:\MOUSE\MOUSE.COM /Y.`

In order to get high with LH, you must have the following three musketeers in your CONFIG.SYS:

`DEVICE=C:\DOS\HIMEM.SYS`
`DEVICE=C:\DOS\EMM386.EXE NOEMS or RAM`
`DOS=UMB or DOS=HIGH,UMB`

Together, they provide access to upper memory so LOADHIGH throw your TSRs up there and out of the way.

For more memories, see *The Complete Idiot's Guide to DOS*, Chapter 20, "Pump Up the RAM!"

MD (MKDIR)

MD Surgically implants another branch (directory) onto the DOS directory tree of life. (Pretty poetic, huh? Not bad for a computer book author.)

When you use the MKDIR command (called just MD by his pals from the 'hood), it creates the new directory as a *subdirectory* of whatever directory happens to be current. For example, if you're currently in the root directory, the new directory will be created off of the root. If you're in the \WORD directory, the new directory is created as a subdirectory of \WORD.

1. Type **CD** and then the directory name under which you want to add the new directory.

For example, to create a directory called BIGFOOT under the directory \SIGHTNGS, change to the SIGHTNGS directory by typing **CD\SIGHTNGS.**

2. Press ⏎Enter.

3. Type **MD.**

4. Press ⎵ Spacebar ⎵.

5. Type the name of the new directory you want to create.

For example, type **MD BIGFOOT.**

6. Press ⏎Enter.

To make more directories, make tracks to *The Complete Idiot's Guide to DOS*, Chapter 13, "Let Your Fingers Do the Walking—Directory Assistance."

MEM

Use this command to tell you the sordid truth about the scandalous way your PC gobbles memory (otherwise known as RAM). Then jump to "More Than You Want to Know About Configuring Your PC," to see what you can do about improving things a bit.

Why should you care about RAM? Well, when you start
a program, the program files are loaded into RAM from
the hard disk. If you run complex programs—or create
large documents—your PC is gonna need *lots of RAM*. So
you better do what you can to make sure your PC uses
what memory it has wisely.

1. Type **MEM**.

2. Press [Spacebar].

3. Type /**P**.

The /P switch stops the results from scrolling off your
screen before you can read them. Useful option for
those of us who flunked out of Evelyn Wood.

4. **(Optional)** Press [Spacebar] and type /**C** to
   display a list of the programs in memory.

   OR

   Press [Spacebar] and type /**F** to display the
   amount of free memory.

5. Press [↵Enter].

Click on a drive letter to check

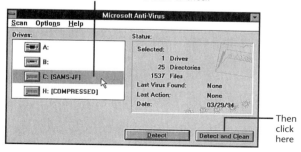

Then
click
here

For information about how to make the most of memory, see *The Complete Idiot's Guide to DOS*, Chapter 20, "Pump Up the RAM!"

MEMMAKER

MemMaker makes changes that optimize (improve) your system's use of memory, helping it "be all that it can be." So just sit back and relax, and let MemMaker do all the hard work for you.

MemMaker is great, but it's not perfect. A PC guru who knows the tricks can optimize your system's memory usage better than MemMaker can. If you want to know more about memory and how to make the most of it, read the section, "More Than You'll Want to Know About Configuring Your PC" later in this book. For even more info, read *10 Minute Guide to Memory Management*. (Watch out: this is a blatant plug for another book I've written.)

1. Exit all programs, including Windows and the DOS Shell.

2. Type **MEMMAKER**.

3. Press ⏎Enter.

4. Press ⏎Enter to select **Express**.

Use the Express option; it's for real people like us. Custom is for geeky-gotta-get-more-RAM-out-of-this-thing-just-to-show-I-can people from the planet RAMbo. If you want to choose Custom, press ⟨ Spacebar ⟩ and then press ⏎Enter.

5. Select **Yes** or **No** when asked if you need expanded memory. To select **No**, simply press ⏎Enter. To select **Yes**, press [Spacebar] and then press ⏎Enter.

If you've got a program which requires expanded memory, it'll tell you right on the box. If you're not sure, just click on **No** in step 5. You can always rerun MemMaker later if you change your mind.

6. Press ⏎Enter. MemMaker restarts your computer.

7. When prompted, press ⏎Enter again. MemMaker tests the new configuration.

8. When asked, select **Yes** if the computer restarted okay or **No** if it didn't.

9. Press ⏎Enter to exit MemMaker.

If you really hate what MemMaker just did to your PC (and you might), type **MEMMAKER** **/UNDO** and press ⏎Enter to undo it.

Can't get enough about memory? Try *The Complete Idiot's Guide to DOS*, Chapter 20, "Pump Up the RAM!"

MENUCOLOR

MENUCOLOR is one of the commands that lets you create a startup menu so you can make choices about what you want to do today, even though you haven't had your second cup of coffee and you're not awake enough to care. Specifically, MENUCOLOR lets you display your newly created startup menu in blazing Technicolor (virtual reality menus will be offered in an upcoming edition of DOS, I'm sure).

Warning: a startup menu is not for the faint of heart, but it's fun once you have it installed. For more menu madness, check out the commands: INCLUDE, MENUDEFAULT, MENUITEM, and SUBMENU, and see the section, "More Than You'll Want to Know About Configuring Your PC" later in this book.

In your CONFIG.SYS:

1. Type **MENUCOLOR=**.

2. Type the color number for the menu text (see the table).

3. Type a comma and the color number for the menu background.

Try This!

For example, to get white text on a blue background, type **MENUCOLOR=7,9**.

Here's a list of colors and their numbers:

Color	Number
Black	0
Blue	1
Green	2
Cyan	3
Red	4
Magenta	5
Brown	6
White	7
Gray	8
Bright Blue	9

Color	Number
Bright Green	10
Bright Cyan	11
Bright Red	12
Bright Magenta	13
Yellow	14
Bright White	15

MENUDEFAULT

If you create a startup menu (see the MENUITEM command), then MENUDEFAULT allows you to select one of your menu options as the "chosen one"—the default menu selection. That way, if the user falls asleep during startup and forgets to chose something from the startup menu, the computer will carry out the commands for the default menu selection.

For more menu mania, check out the commands: INCLUDE, MENUCOLOR, MENUITEM, and SUBMENU, and see the section, "More Than You'll Want to Know About Configuring Your PC" later in this book.

In your CONFIG.SYS, *after* the MENUITEM commands (which define the selections which appear on the startup menu), type this command:

1. Type **MENUDEFAULT=**.

2. Type the label of the menu selection you want to use as the default.

This label has to match one of the labels used earlier, in the MENUITEM commands.

3. **(Optional)** Type a comma (**,**) and press the [Spacebar]. Then type the amount of time (in seconds) that you want the menu to sit around and wait for the user to make a choice.

Suppose you've set up a menu system which gives the user a choice between basic configuration (for everyday duties) and games configuration (for fun). Further suppose that you want to make the basic configuration the choice of champions (the default), but you want to give the user ten seconds of bliss to consider overriding you and choosing to have fun with games instead. Type this:

```
[MENU]
MENUITEM=BASIC, Basic Configuration
MENUITEM=GAMES, Games Configuration
MENUDEFAULT=BASIC, 15.
```

Of course, these are not the only commands you'll need to create a complete menu. See MENUITEM first for more help, then check out the section, "More Than You'll Want to Know About Configuring Your PC."

MENUITEM

MENUITEM is used in the CONFIG.SYS to set up the actual choices presented on your startup menu. That way, if you don't feel like working (i.e. your boss is out of town) you can select "Games" from the startup menu and your PC will be ready to rock and roll (at least until your boss comes back).

For midnight menu madness, check out the commands: INCLUDE, MENUCOLOR, MENUITEM, and SUBMENU, and see the "More Than You'll Want to Know About Configuring Your PC" section later in this book.

Somewhere near the beginning of your CONFIG.SYS file, insert these commands:

1. Type **[MENU]** and press ↵Enter.

You create a menu by entering a block of commands under the header **[MENU]**. The commands you enter under this "flag" include things like the MENUITEM command shown here, along with optional thingies such as MENUCOLOR, MENUDEFAULT, and SUBMENU. After you define a menu, you define the commands you want to happen when each menu item is chosen, again by including a header thingy followed by a series of CONFIG.SYS commands. Stay tuned for more exciting news on menus.

2. Type **MENUITEM=**.

3. Type a label for this menu selection.

For example, type **MENUITEM=NETWK**.

4. (**Optional**) Type a comma (**,**) followed by a description of this menu item.

Suppose you want to set up a menu system which gives the user a choice between basic configuration (for

everyday duties) and network configuration (for connecting to the company network system and causing
havoc). Type this:

```
[MENU]
MENUITEM=BASIC, Basic Configuration
MENUITEM=NETWK, Network Configuration
```

Later in the CONFIG.SYS, you group together the
configuration commands you want carried out with each
choice, by placing labels (called *headers*) in the file to
identify them (kinda like the labels your Mom used to
sew in your underwear to identify it). For example:

```
[BASIC]
C:\DOS\HIMEM.SYS
C:\DOS\EMM386.EXE NOEMS
DOS=HIGH,UMB
FILES=30
PATH=C:\DOS;C:\WINDOWS

[NETWK]
C:\DOS\HIMEM.SYS
FILES=45
C:\NET\NETWORK.SYS
PATH=C:\DOS;C:\NET
```

In this example, only the commands under one section
(BASIC or NETWK) are carried out. Note that the headers
match what you used in the MENUITEM commands
earlier in the CONFIG.SYS—an important fact if you
want your menu to do anything but just sit there and
look pretty. This is just one way to set up a menu. For
the whole picture, check out the section "More Than
You'll Want to Know About Configuring Your PC" later
in this book.

MODE

When you're especially bored, you can use the MODE
command to play around with the setup of certain
devices such as your modem or your printer.

MODE: Checking the Status of System Devices

1. Type **MODE**.
2. Press [Spacebar].
3. Type ¦**MORE**.
4. Press [↵Enter].

You'll see some information describing the status of each of the ports: the LPT ports (printer stuff) and COM ports (modem stuff). All of the information is certified "unintelligible" and guaranteed to "cause snooze city," so be careful when using this command.

MODE: Redirecting Default Printing to a Serial Port

In the unlikely event you have a DOS program that sends all its output to the first printer port (LPT1) without giving you a choice, and you have a serial printer (such as a Diablo 630 or a daisywheel printer) which is attached to another port (COM1), type these commands to configure it. For advice about what settings to use, see your DOS documentation.

1. Type **MODE**.
2. Press [Spacebar].
3. Type **COM**.
4. Type the number of the COM port you're configuring, followed by a colon.

For example, type **MODE COM1:**

5. Type a baud rate (see table below). Type a comma (,).

Type . . .	To set baud rate to . . .
11	110 baud
15	150 baud
30	300 baud
60	600 baud
12	1200 baud
24	2400 baud
48	4800 baud
96	9600 baud
19	19,200 baud

6. Type a parity (see table below). Then type another comma (**,**).

Type . . .	To set parity to . . .
E	Even
M	Mark
N	None
O	Odd

7. Specify the number of data bits (5–8). Then type another comma (**,**).

8. Specify the number of stop bits (1, 1.5, or 2). Add a comma (**,**).

9. Specify a Retry mode (see table below).

Type . . .	To set Retry to . . .
E	Send error message if port is busy.
B	Send "busy" if port is busy.
N	Do nothing if port is busy.
P	Continue trying if port is busy.
R	Send "ready" if port is busy.

10. Press ⏎Enter.

Don't let these numbers scare you. A common setting is **MODE COM1:96,N,8,1,P**. If in doubt, try this setting.

After you've issued the above command, you need to type another command to tell DOS to send printer stuff to the serial port, and not to the parallel port which it normally uses. Follow these steps:

1. Type **MODE**.

2. Press ⸤ Spacebar ⸥.

3. Type **LPT**.

4. Type the parallel port number (for example, **1**).

5. Type an equals sign (=).

6. Type **COM**.

7. Type the serial port number (for example, **2**).

8. Press ⏎Enter.

For example, to redirect LPT1: to COM2:, type **MODE LPT1=COM2**.

To cancel a redirection:

1. Type **MODE**.
2. Press ⌊ Spacebar ⌋.
3. Type **LPT**.
4. Type the parallel port number.
5. Press ⌊⏎Enter⌋.

MORE

Clunky old DOS often forgets that the people who use it are not computers (and therefore, can't read information that scrolls off the screen faster than a speeding bullet). With some commands, such as DIR, DOS is thoughtful enough to provide a switch (/P) for just such occasions, but not often. When the /P switch doesn't work on a command, send for MORE.

1. Type the DOS command. Press ⌊ Spacebar ⌋.
2. Type the pipe symbol (¦).

The pipe symbol is sometimes a tough guy to find. Look for him on the backslash (\) key.

3. Press ⌊ Spacebar ⌋ and type **MORE**.
4. Press ⌊⏎Enter⌋.

The DOS command is carried out, and the results are displayed on-screen. When the screen gets full, it stops and prints the message:

— More —

at the bottom of the screen. Press <u>↵Enter</u> when you want
to see more.

For example, to read the README.TXT file because
the documentation tells you to do it before you install
your new !!500 program wrong, type this:

TYPE README.TXT ¦ MORE

Want to know MORE? See *The Complete Idiot's Guide to
DOS*, Chapter 13, "Let Your Fingers Do the Walking—
Directory Assistance."

MOVE

MOVE enables you to move files from one disk or
directory to another in fewer steps than with the clumsy
COPY command. (Moving files is the same as copying
them to a new location and then deleting them from the
old location.)

You can also rename a directory (though I'm not sure
why you'd want to) with the MOVE command.

If you try to move a file on top of an existing file with
the same name, you'll be asked if you really, really
want to do this. If you do, press <u>Y</u> and then <u>↵Enter</u>.
If you don't, press <u>N</u> instead.

MOVE: Moving a Single File

1. Type **MOVE**.

2. Press <u>Spacebar</u>.

3. Type the file's current location (like this:
   drive:\directory).

4. Type the filename (like this: *filename.ext*).

5. Press ⎵ Spacebar .

6. Type the location to move to (like this: *drive:\directory*).

7. Press ⏎Enter.

For example, to move the file WK2HARD.WK4 from the \123 directory to \SECRET\HIDDEN directory so Joey can't find the file while you're on vacation and therefore trash it in his usual bungling way, type this:

```
MOVE C:\123\WK2HARD.WK4 C:\SECRET\HIDDEN
```

For more info, get a MOVE on to *The Complete Idiot's Guide to DOS*, Chapter 11, "Standing at the Copier, Copying Files."

MOVE: Moving Multiple Files

1. Type **MOVE**.

2. Press ⎵ Spacebar .

3. Type the current location (like this: *drive:\directory*).

4. Type the wildcard file specification.

For example, to move all the files, type ***.***. To move all files that end in DOC, type ***.DOC**; to move all files that begin with M, type **M*.***. For more ways to get wild, see the section, "The Least You Need to Know About DOS" at the front of this book.

5. Press ⎵ Spacebar .

6. Type the location to move to (like this:
   drive:\directory).

7. Press ⏎Enter.

MOVE: Renaming a Directory

Hate the name PROJECTS? Well, just rename that
directory something less threatening like: STUFF2DO or
IFIEVERFINDTHETIME (OK, so you can't use more than
eight letters when naming a directory—gotta admit it's
better than PROJECTS, though.)

1. Type **MOVE**.

2. Press ⌷ Spacebar ⌷.

3. Type the current name of the directory (like this:
   drive:\directory).

4. Press ⌷ Spacebar ⌷.

5. Type the new name for the directory (like this:
   drive:\directory).

6. Press ⏎Enter.

Try This!

For example, to rename the directory PRESLEY to
JACKSON, type:

MOVE C:\PRESLEY C:\JACKSON

Curious about all this directory business? Check out *The
Complete Idiot's Guide to DOS*, Chapter 13, "Let Your
Fingers Do the Walking—Directory Assistance."

MS AntiVirus, DOS Version (MSAV)

A virus is a program that infects your computer in
various ways, such as changing your files, damaging

your disks, and preventing your computer from start-ing—fun stuff like that. Some viruses don't do any actual damage; they just display funny messages or pictures. But they are still annoying; especially when they wait until the exact moment you begin your client demo to display something charming like "Stuff Happens." MS AntiVirus allows you to detect and remove computer viruses and other things that go bump in the night.

There's also a Windows version of this program; if you use Windows, pass Go, collect $200, and skip to the next section.

For 24-hour protection from bad-guy viruses, see VSAFE. For protection from VSAFE false alarms, don't use it.

1. Exit all programs, including Windows and the DOS Shell.

2. Reboot your computer with your emergency diskette.

An emergency diskette is one which contains a copy of DOS (it's bootable), and which (hopefully) hasn't been contaminated by the virus which is happily raising havoc on your PC right now. See FORMAT for more info.

3. Type: **MSAV** and press [Spacebar].

4. Type **/A** and press [Spacebar].

   OR

   If you're connected to a network, type **/L** and press [Spacebar].

The /A switch says to check all drives for viruses, such as C and D. The /L switch limits the search to drives on your system, and not the network drives, thank you very much.

5. Type **/C** to specify you want any viruses removed that are found.

   OR

   To check for viruses without removing them, type **/S**.

6. **(Optional)** To create a report of all viruses found, press [Spacebar] and type **/R**.

The report is called MSAV.RPT, and it's placed in the root directory. To see it, type:

TYPE C:\MSAV.RPT ¦ MORE and press [↵Enter].

7. Press [↵Enter].

8. Wait for MS AntiVirus to scan your hard disk.

9. Press [F3] to quit.

Wake up fine every morning with a stiff cup of coffee and a good virus scan. Just add this to your AUTOEXEC.BAT:

MSAV /N

If you're attached to a network, don't forget the /L switch: **MSAV /N /L.**

MSAV only checks the current status of your hard disk. For 24-hour protection, see VSAFE.

Got a virus that just won't quit? Take two aspirin, then see *The Complete Idiot's Guide to DOS*, Chapter 18, "Virus Got You Down?"

MS AntiVirus, Windows Version (MWAV)

If you think your computer's acting strange, don't assume it's a computer virus. You may be using a program that's not installed properly, or your equipment may be planning a permanent vacation. With MS AntiVirus, you can test your system for viruses before you call out the National Guard.

When you suspect a problem, perform these steps (from within Microsoft Windows):

1. Double-click on the **Microsoft Tools** group icon

Microsoft Tools

2. Double-click on the **AntiVirus** icon.

Anti-Virus

Click on a drive letter to check

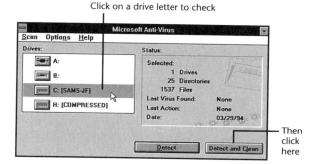

Then click here

3. Click on the drive letter(s) you want to check.

4. Click on **Detect and Clean**.

5. Wait while MS AntiVirus checks your hard disk.

6. If asked, click on **Update** to update the information on a file (if for example, you know that the file was changed legitimately) or, if you suspect a virus, click on **Clean** to attempt to remove it.

7. When finished, click on **Scan** and then click on **Exit Anti-Virus**.

Stuffy head, fever, and a computer virus? Well, take two aspirin, then check out *The Complete Idiot's Guide to DOS,* Chapter 18, "Virus Got You Down?"

MS Backup, DOS Version (MSBACKUP)

MS Backup copies the files on your hard disk onto a series of diskettes, so that you can restore them later on if the originals get damaged in some way, like when your hard disk goes on "permanent vacation" and takes your files along with it. You will want to back up your hard disk frequently to guard against data loss.

MS Backup comes in a version that you can run from
Windows. See the next section for details.

For more info on backups, see *The Complete Idiot's Guide
to DOS*, Chapter 14, "Backing Up Your Hard Disk."

MS Backup (DOS): Starting from the DOS Prompt

1. Type **MSBACKUP**.

2. Press (↵Enter).

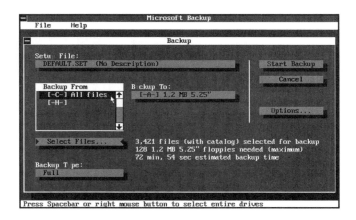

MS Backup (DOS): Exiting

When you're done, bid the MS Backup program a fond
adieu, until next time, hasta la vista, baby:

1. Return to the Main menu by clicking on **Cancel**.

2. Click on **Quit**.

MS Backup (DOS): Backing Up Your Data

The first time you run MS Backup, you must perform a compatiblity test which determines the diskette drive to be used. If you haven't performed a compatibility test yet, skip to "MS Backup (DOS): Performing a Compatibility Test" and then come back. I'll wait. The next time you want to do a backup, you'll get the main screen right away, without having to go through the testing rigamorole.

Once you've gone through the compatibility test trauma, follow these steps to perform a complete backup of your hard disk.

1. Start MS Backup as usual.

2. Click on **Backup**.

You can save your selections in a setup file and reuse it every time the need to do another backup hits you. See "MS Backup (DOS): Saving Your Selections" in this section.

3. Under **Backup From**, right-click on the drive you want to back up. Repeat for additional drives.

Right-click, not surprisingly, means to click with the right mouse button. Now you know.

4. **(Optional)** Select another diskette drive to backup to by clicking on **Backup To**, clicking on a selection, then clicking on **OK**.

If you can tear yourself away from the fascinating process of watching an entire hard disk being backed up, and you'd like to backup only your most important files, see "MS Backup (DOS): Selecting Files for Backup or Restore" later in this section.

5. **(Optional)** Change the type of backup by clicking on **Backup Type**, selecting a type, then clicking on **OK**.

A *full* backup backs up all files you select. An *incremental* backup backs up all files you select, that have been changed since the last backup (of any kind). That means that if you ever need to restore your entire hard disk, you not only need the diskettes from your last full backup, but the diskettes from *every incremental backup* you did after it.

A *differential* backup saves you some disks, by backing up all the files that have been changed since the last full backup, even if they were backed up already by an incremental or differential backup. This is cool because you don't have to keep the diskettes for each differential backup you do between full backups—only the most recent set.

6. Click on **Start Backup**.

7. Insert disks when prompted and click **Continue** if necessary.

8. When the backup is complete, click on **OK**.

MS Backup (DOS): Performing a Compatibility Test

The first time you start MS Backup, you'll be greeted by a message which says you have to perform a compatibility test to ensure that MS Backup will work reliably with your system. Get a #2 pencil and be sure to press firmly (just kidding):

1. Start MS Backup if you haven't already.

2. Click on **Start Configuration**.

3. Click **OK**.

4. Click on **Start Test**.

5. Click **OK**.

6. Wait for the processor speed test to finish.

7. Click on **Start Test**.

8. Wait for the compatibility test to finish.

9. Click on **Continue**.

10. Click on the diskette type you want to use for backups, then click on **OK**.

11. Locate two blank diskettes (of the specified type) that don't contain any data you need.

12. Place one diskette in the specified drive, then click on **Continue**.

If your diskette is not as empty as you thought it was, either replace it and click on **Retry**, or let the test overwrite whatever's on the diskette by clicking on **Overwrite**.

13. When prompted, remove the diskette and insert the second diskette.

14. When the backup is complete, click on **OK**.

15. Place the first backup diskette back into the drive, and click on **Continue**.

16. When prompted, remove the first diskette and insert the second diskette.

17. Click on **OK** when the compare process is finished.

18. Click on **OK** to confirm that the test was successful, then click on **Save** to save the configuration.

MS Backup (DOS): Rebuilding a Catalog

A backup catalog lists the files you backed up, along with their last known locations. If yours has gone the way of the Sears catalog, you can reconstruct it from the backup disk. Follow these steps.

1. Start MSBackup as usual.

2. Click on **Restore**.

3. Click on **Catalog**.

4. Click on **Rebuild**.

5. Select the site where the backup catalog was last seen, then click on **OK**.

For example, if you backed up your files onto drive A, select that drive.

6. Insert diskettes as prompted. When the backup catalog has been rebuilt, click on **OK**.

MS Backup (DOS): Restoring Your Data

Okay, the worst has happened. You try to open an important document, and you're greeted with **Data error reading file**. Or worse yet, all the files on your hard disk have somehow been eaten by the latest computer virus. What do you do? Well, you thank your lucky stars that you did a backup, then you just sit back, relax, and restore them. The restoring process copies the good versions of your files onto your hard disk, to replace the damaged versions.

1. Start MS Backup as usual.

2. Click on **Restore**.

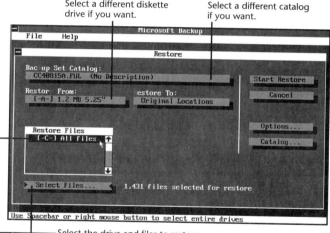

Select a different diskette drive if you want.

Select a different catalog if you want.

Select the drive and files to restore.

3. (Optional) If you want to select another catalog, click on **Select Backup Set Catalog**. Click on a catalog, then click on **Load**.

If there's no catalog listed, you'll have to reconstruct it. Get a hammer and some nails, then refer to "MS Backup (DOS): Rebuilding a Catalog."

4. **(Optional)** If you want to restore from some other diskette drive, click on **Restore From**. Click on a drive, then click **OK**.

5. Under **Restore Files**, click *with the right mouse button* on a drive. The words **All Files** will appear next to the drive.

6. **(Optional)** If you don't want to restore all of the files that were originally backed up, click on **Select Files**.

Refer to the section "MS Backup (DOS): Selecting Files to Backup or Restore" to learn how to select the files you want to join your restore party.

7. Click on **Start Restore**.

8. Insert diskettes as prompted.

9. When the restoring process is complete, click on **OK**.

MS Backup (DOS): Saving Your Selections

Since doing a backup is about as much fun as watching grass grow, why not make the process as painless as possible? Make your selections once, then save them in a file which you can reuse whenever you feel like doing a backup.

1. Select the drive, backup type, and/or particular files you want to back up on a regular basis.

2. Click on **File**.

3. Click on **Save Setup As**.

4. Type a filename.

You can use eight whole characters here. For example, type **WRKFILES**.

5. Type a description.

For example, type **Work project files**.

6. Click on **Save**.

Later on, you can select a setup file from the Backup window by clicking on **Setup File**, then clicking on a setup *with the right mouse button.* Click on **Open**. Then you're ready to start the backup.

MS Backup (DOS): Selecting Files to Back Up or Restore

Unless you're looking for a way to kill a few hours so you don't have to start that big project you've been putting off for weeks, why back up program files that never change? Instead of backing up the entire hard disk, just back up the files you create. If you place your files in a particular directory, you can back up just that directory. If you don't, you can back up selected files located all over the hard disk—whatever works best for your situation.

You can use these same techniques to restore selected files. For example, the files that Uncle Billy accidentally trashed when you let him use the computer to play Killer Mutant Ants From Planet Orkin.

All the files in this directory will be restored.

Only files marked with a checkmark will be restored.

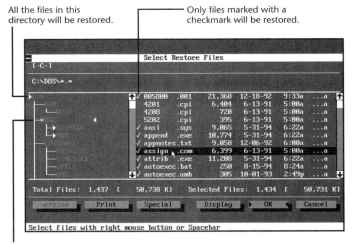

Some of the files in this directory will be restored.

From the Backup or Restore Window:

1. Click on **Select Files**.

2. Select the files you want to backup or restore:

   ➤ To select all the files on the entire drive, double-click on the root directory.

The *root directory* is located at the top of the listing, because it's the big boss directory that all the other directories branch off from. When you perform step 2, a triangle appears next to the root. To deselect all the files on a drive, double-click on the root again. The triangle goes away.

   ➤ To select an entire directory, click on it *with the right mouse button*. A triangle appears in front of selected directories.

   ➤ To select a single file, click on it *with the right mouse button*. A check mark appears in front of selected files.

➤ To include all files with a given extension or wild card pattern, click on **Include**. Under **Path**, type the directory you want to affect: *directory*. Under **File**, type a file specification: *filespec*. Click on **OK**.

For example, to include all files with a .DOC extension, type ***.DOC** under File. If you're feeling generous and you want to include all .DOC files on the entire disk, type **C:** under Path, and click on **Include All Subdirectories**.

➤ To exclude all files with a particular extension or wild card pattern, click on **Exclude**. Under Path, type the directory you want to affect: *directory*. Under File, type a file specification: *filespec*. Click on **OK**.

From this dialog box, click on **Edit Include/ Exclude List** to see who you've invited so far. This is a good idea, since you won't believe how many files try to crash the party when you're not looking. You can then remove any files selected by mistake without starting over.

➤ To exclude files with particular attributes, such as hidden or system files, click on **Special**. Click on the attributes you want to exclude, then click on **OK**.

➤ To exclude files in a specified date range, click on **Special**. Press Ⓕ, then type the beginning date. Press Ⓣ, then type the ending date. Click on **OK**.

Try This!

For example, type **10-16-94**.

3. Click on **OK** to return to the Backup or Restore window. Start the backup or restore by clicking on **Start Backup** or **Start Restore**.

MS Backup, Windows Version (MWBACKUP)

MS Backup copies the files on your hard disk onto a series of diskettes, so that you can restore them later on if the originals get damaged in some way, like when your hard disk goes on "permanent vacation" and takes your files along with it. You will want to back up your hard disk frequently to guard against data loss.

Tip

Doing backups in Windows is more convenient, so of course, there's a catch: you won't be able to back up any files that are currently in use. So if you're backing up your entire hard disk, you'll miss some important files (like all the ones Windows use). MS Backup comes in a version you can run from the DOS prompt. See the previous section for details.

Want to know more about backups? See *The Complete Idiot's Guide to DOS*, Chapter 14, "Backing Up Your Hard Disk."

MS Backup (Windows): Starting

To start MS Backup for Windows:

1. Double click on the **Microsoft Tools** program group icon:
Microsoft Tools

2. Double-click on the **MS Backup** icon:

Select the drive whose files you want to back up.   Click here to start the backup.

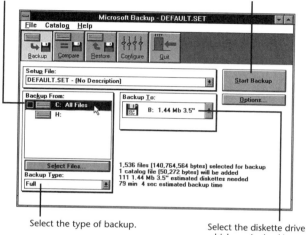

Select the type of backup.

Select the diskette drive to which you're backing up.

MS Backup (Windows): Exiting

When you're done, bid the MS Backup program a fond farewell:

1. Click on **File**.

2. Click on **Exit**.

3. (**Optional**) If you want to save changes you made to the configuration of MS Backup, click on **Save Configuration**.

4. (**Optional**) If you want to save your selections as the default, click on **Save Settings In Default.Set**.

5. Click on **OK**.

MS Backup (Windows): Backing Up Your Data

The first time you run MS Backup, you must perform a compatibility test (don't worry—it's multiple choice). If you haven't performed a compatibility test yet, skip to "Performing a Compatibility Test" then come back. I'll wait. The next time you want to do a backup, you'll get the main screen right away, without having to go through the testing rigamorole.

When you've made it through compatibility test purgatory, use these steps to perform a complete backup of your hard disk:

1. Start MS Backup as usual.

2. Click on **Backup**.

You can save your selections in a setup file and reuse it every time the need to do another backup hits you. See "MS Backup (Windows): Saving Your Selections" in this section.

3. Under **Backup From**, right-click on the drive you want to back up. Repeat for additional drives.

4. (Optional) Select a different diskette drive to back up to by clicking on the down arrow next to **Backup To** and making a selection.

If you can tear yourself away from the fascinating process of watching an entire hard disk being backed up, and you'd like to back up only your most important files, see "MS Backup (Windows): Selecting Files for Backup or Restore" later in this section.

5. (Optional) Change the type of backup by clicking on the down arrow next to **Backup Type**, and selecting a type.

A *full* backup backs up all files you select. An *incremental* backup backs up all files you select, that have been changed since the last backup (of any kind). That means that if you ever need to restore your entire hard disk, you not only need the diskettes from your last full backup, but the diskettes from *every incremental backup* you did after it.

A *differential* backup saves you some disks, by backing up all the files that have been changed since the last full backup, even if they were backed up already by an incremental or differential backup. This is cool because you don't have to keep the diskettes for each differential backup you do between full backups—only the most recent set.

6. Click on **Start Backup**.

7. Insert disks when prompted and click **Continue** if necessary.

8. When the backup is complete, click on **OK**.

MS Backup (Windows): Performing a Compatibility Test

The first time you start MS Backup for Windows, you'll be stopped in your tracks by a message which says you have to perform a compatibility test to ensure that MS Backup will work reliably with your system. And you thought you were done with tests when you graduated from high school:

1. Start MS Backup as usual.

2. When you get the message that you need to configure, click on **Yes**.

3. Remove all diskettes from the drives.

4. Click on the diskette type you want to use for backups, then click on **OK**.

5. Locate two blank diskettes (of the specified type) that don't contain any data you need. Place one diskette in the specified drive.

If your diskette is not as empty as you thought it was, either replace it and click on **Retry**, or let the test overwrite whatever's on the diskette by clicking on **Overwrite**.

6. When prompted, remove the diskette and insert the second diskette.

7. When the backup is complete, place the first backup diskette back into the drive, and click on **OK**.

8. When prompted, remove the first diskette and insert the second diskette.

9. Click on **OK** when the comparison process is finished.

10. Click on **OK** to confirm that the test was successful.

MS Backup (Windows): Rebuilding a Catalog

A backup catalog lists the files you backed up, along with their last known locations. If yours has gone the way of the Sears catalog, you can reconstruct it from the backup disk. Follow these steps.

1. Start MS Backup as usual.

2. Click on **Restore**.

3. Click on **Catalog**.

4. Click on **Rebuild**.

5. Under **From**, select the drive used for the backup diskettes, then click on **OK**.

Try This!

For example, if you backed up your files onto drive A, select that drive.

6. Insert disks as prompted. When the backup catalog has been rebuilt, click on **OK**.

MS Backup (Windows): Restoring Your Data

Okay, the worst has happened. You try to open an important document, and you're greeted with **Data error reading file**. Or worse yet, all the files on your hard disk have somehow been eaten by the latest computer virus. What do you do? Well, you thank your lucky stars that you did a backup, then you just sit back, relax, and restore them. The restore process copies the good versions of your files onto your hard disk, to replace the damaged versions.

1. Start MS Backup as usual.

2. Click on **Restore**.

Select a different diskette drive to restore from, if you want.

Select a different catalog if you want.

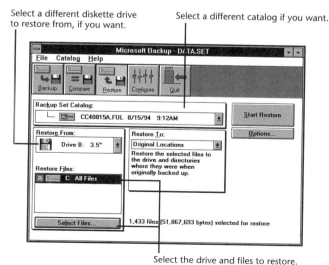

Select the drive and files to restore.

3. **(Optional)** The catalog of files that were backed up most recently is loaded for you automatically. If you want to select another catalog, click on the down arrow next to **Backup Set Catalog**. Then click on a catalog.

If there's no catalog listed, you'll have to reconstruct it. Get a hammer and some nails, then refer to "MS Backup (Windows): Rebuilding a Catalog."

4. **(Optional)** If you want to restore from some other diskette drive, click on the down arrow next to **Restore From**. Then click on a different diskette drive.

5. Under **Restore Files**, click *with the right mouse button* on a drive. The words **All Files** will appear next to the drive.

6. **(Optional)** If you don't want to restore your files to the directories or drives from which they were originally backed up, then click on the down arrow next to **Restore To**.

   Then select another location. During the restoring process, you'll be prompted to supply the name of the mystery directory or drive to which you want to restore your files.

7. **(Optional)** If you don't want to restore all of the files that were originally backed up, click on **Select Files**.

Refer to the section "MS Backup (Windows): Selecting Files to Backup or Restore" to learn how to select the files you want to join your restore party.

8. Click on **Start Restore**. Insert diskettes as prompted. When the restore process is complete, click on **OK**.

MS Backup (Windows): Saving Your Selections

Since doing a backup is about as much fun as watching grass grow, why not make the process as painless as possible? Make your selections once, then save them in a file which you can reuse whenever you feel like doing a backup.

1. Select the drive, backup type, and/or particular files you want to back up on a regular basis.

2. Click on **File**.

3. Click on **Save Setup As**.

4. Type a filename.

You can type eight whole characters here. For example, type **WRKFILES**.

5. Type a description.

For example, type **Work project files**.

6. Click on **OK**.

Later on, you can select a setup file from the Backup window by clicking on **Setup File**. From the drop-down list, click on a setup file to use. Now you're ready to start the backup.

MS Backup (Windows): Selecting Files to Back Up or Restore

Unless you're looking for a way to kill a few hours at work, why back up program files which never change? Instead of backing up the entire hard disk, just back up the files you create. If you place your files in a particular directory, you can back up just that directory. If you don't, you can back up selected files located all over the hard disk—whatever works best for your situation.

You can use these same techniques to restore selected files. For example, the files that Uncle Billy accidentally trashed when you let him use the computer to play Killer Mutant Ants From Planet Orkin.

All the files in this directory will be restored.

Only some of the files in this directory will be restored.

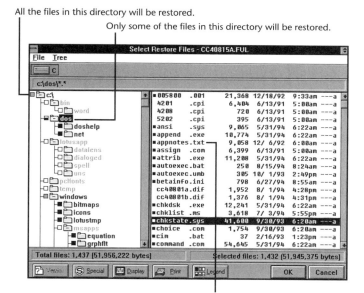

Only files marked with a box will be restored.

From the Backup or Restore Window:

1. Click on **Select Files**.

2. Select the files you want to back up or restore:

   ➤ To select all the files on the entire drive, double-click on the root directory.

For example, click on **C:**. The **root directory** is located at the top of the listing, because it's the big boss directory that all the other directories branch off from. A black box appears next to the root. To deselect all the files on a drive, double-click on the root again. The big bad box goes away.

There are other boxes you might see; click on **Legend** to view a complete listing of the best box nominees.

   ➤ To select an entire directory, click on it *with the right mouse button*. A black box appears in front of selected directories.

   ➤ To select a single file, click on it *with the right mouse button*. A black box appears in front of selected files.

   ➤ To exclude files with particular attributes, such as hidden or system files, click on **Special**. Click on the attributes of the files you want to exclude, then click on **OK**.

   ➤ To exclude files in a specified date range, click on **Special**. Click on the **Apply Range** checkbox. Type the beginning date. Then type the ending date. Click on **OK**.

For example, type **10-16-94**.

3. Click on **OK** to return to the Backup or Restore window. Start the backup or restore by clicking on **Start Backup** or **Start Restore**.

Microsoft Diagnostics (MSD)

Makes your PC open its tongue and say, "Ahhhh." With MSD, you can discover all sorts of neat things you didn't know about your PC, such as how much memory it has, what type of video adapter you're using, and your DOS version—essential stuff you need to know to install programs, diagnose problems, and bore people at parties.

Be warned: most of this stuff has been declared dreadfully dull by the Surgeon General's office, and prolonged exposure should be avoided.

1. Exit all programs, including Windows and the DOS Shell.

2. Type **MSD**.

3. Press ⏎Enter.

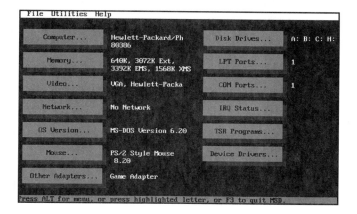

4. To see more info on a particular topic, click on its button. To return to the main screen, press (Esc).

For example, to see what type of CPU this puppy uses, click on **Computer**.

5. When you're done poking, press (F3) to exit.

Got troubles that just won't quit? See *The Complete Idiot's Guide to DOS*, Chapter 28, "DOS 6-Something to the Rescue!"

MSD: Printing Information

If your brain works anything like mine, you probably won't remember everything MSD tells you about your computer. Instead of memorizing this stuff, just print it out and keep it handy in case a nerd walks by and asks you, "So, what IRQs are you using?"

1. Start MSD as usual.

2. Click on **File**.

3. Click on **Print Report**.

4. **(Optional)** Click on items you don't want to print to deselect them. (Items which *are* selected appear with an X in their checkbox.)

5. **(Optional)** Change the printer port to print to if you want.

You can save this stuff permanently in a file if you'd like, and then use the TYPE command when necessary to view its contents.

6. Click on **OK**.

MSD: Testing Your Printer

MSD now comes with 25% less sugar, and a neat printer test program.

1. Start MSD as usual.

2. Click on **Utilities**.

3. Click on **Test Printer**.

4. **(Optional)** Select your printer type.

5. **(Optional)** Select a different printer port if necessary.

6. Turn your printer on, and click on **OK**.

MSD: Viewing Configuration Files

With MSD, you can sneak a peak at your configuration files (such as the AUTOEXEC.BAT)—no crowbars necessary!

1. Start MSD as usual.

2. Click on **File**.

3. Click on the file you want to view.

For example, click on **CONFIG.SYS**.

4. **(Optional)** To see more of the file, press ⌈PgDn⌉. To see a previous section of the file, press ⌈PgUp⌉.

5. When you're done, click on **OK**.

PATH

You use PATH to set up a search list of possible suspects (directories) to help DOS find all of its commands. Dumb as it sounds, without a PATH, you might see the error, "Bad command or file name" when entering a perfectly ordinary DOS command.

You also use PATH so DOS can locate your favorite programs (such as Windows) whenever you type the command to start them.

PATH's place is in the AUTOEXEC.BAT file. For more info on this and other fascinating things you can edit, see "Hacking Away at Files With the DOS Editor" later in this book.

In your AUTOEXEC.BAT file:

1. Type **PATH=**.

2. Type a drive/directory to be included (like this: *drive:\directory*).

3. **(Optional)** To include another drive/directory, type a semicolon (**;**) and repeat step 2.

For example, type:

```
PATH=C:\DOS;C:\WINDOWS;C:\UTILTIES;C:\BATCH
```

Don't get priggy and try to include all your programs in the PATH statement. Just include DOS, Windows (if you use it), your network directory (if you use one), and any DOS programs you use from the prompt and not from within Windows or the Shell.

Want to know more? Beat a path over to *The Complete Idiot's Guide to DOS*, Chapter 4, "May DOS Take Your Order, Please?".

PATH: Displaying the Current Path

1. Type **PATH**.

2. Press ⏎Enter).

If you see the words **No path**, then you haven't set one up. Sniff.

PATH: Canceling the Path

1. Type **PATH**.

2. Type a semicolon (**;**).

3. Press ⏎Enter).

To reset your path, type it all in again (yech), or if it's set up in your AUTOEXEC.BAT, restart your computer.

PAUSE

Within a batch file, this is the pause that refreshes (or at least waits while the user goes to get some refreshment).

When a PAUSE command is reached in a batch file, it displays:

```
Press any key to continue...
```

The batch file then takes a siesta until the user wakes up, notices that processing has stopped, and presses a key to get it going again.

> To learn more about the batch file birthing process, see "Hacking Away at Files With the DOS Editor" later in this book.

Make a message appear on-screen with the ECHO command.

```
     Please insert a new diskette, then let me know when
     you're ready. Take your time; I'll wait.

   Press any key to continue . . .
```

Get your batch file to wait for the user with the PAUSE command.

In a batch file:

1. Insert the commands you want to happen before the system pauses.

2. Type **PAUSE**.

3. Continue with additional batch file commands.

> You might want to display a message such as "Change diskettes now." before you insert the PAUSE command in a batch file. To display messages (helpful or otherwise) in a batch file, see ECHO.

POWER

The POWER command helps you save your laptop's battery charge so it doesn't poop out at 20,000 feet. It performs this bit of magic by conserving battery strength when programs are on coffee breaks, hanging out at the copier, or basically not doing anything special.

How much battery life you actually end up saving with the POWER command depends on your portable, and whether it follows a standard called the APM or Advanced Power Management—but it could be as high as 25% (or as low as 5%). Bottom line: the POWER command won't change your life, but using it could give you that critical 10 minutes you need to finish a big project and then save it.

You place the POWER command in your CONFIG.SYS. Unless you can convince some fool to do it for you, check out the section, "Hacking Away at Files With the DOS Editor" later in this book for more help.

Curious about all this POWER? Check out *The Complete Idiot's Guide to DOS*, Chapter 25, "It's a Portable PC World!"

POWER: Installing POWER

On a line in your CONFIG.SYS:

1. Type `DEVICE=C:\DOS\POWER.EXE`.

2. **(Optional)** To force POWER to conserve as much power as possible, even if it cuts into performance, press ⌷ Spacebar ⌷ and type `ADV:MAX`.

POWER: Changing the Power Conservation Level

You've got the power to change the power conservation level later on if you want, by typing one of these two commands at the DOS prompt:

`POWER ADV:MIN` (for minimum conservation)

or

`POWER ADV:REG` (for regular conservation)

POWER: Checking Your Power Consumption

No one wants to find out that the needle on the gas guage is stuck, and that they are about to run out of gas 40 miles from the nearest gas station. So check the power consumption on your laptop from time to time.

1. Type **POWER**.

2. Press ⏎Enter. You'll see a listing showing you what's what:

```
Power Management Status
— — — — — — — — — —

Setting = ADV: REG
CPU: idle 45% of time.
AC Line Status: OFFLINE
Battery status: High
Battery life (%):
100
```

If you see a number under 35%, you should probably shut down, because power will start dropping off pretty rapidly.

If you don't see anything at all, you're probably not running on batteries (oops!) or your PC doesn't conform to the APM standards (a nonconformist computer—yech).

PRINT

PRINT prints a text file or files while you *don't* wait—it prints in the background, while you get the complete and utter joy of continuing to work.

1. Type **PRINT**.

2. Press 〔 Spacebar 〕.

3. Type the location of the file you want to print (like this: *drive:\directory*).

4. Type the name of the file you want to print.

5. Press 〔↵Enter〕.

6. If you see Name of list device [PRN]:, press 〔↵Enter〕.

For example, to print the file MYTEXT.DOC in the C:\DATA directory, type **PRINT C:\DATA\MYTEXT.DOC**. To print all the DOC files, type **PRINT C:\DATA*.DOC**.

PRINT: Canceling a Print Job

Everyone has a right to change his or her mind (just look at the foreign policy of the last five presidents). If you want to cancel the file being printed:

1. Type **PRINT**.

2. Press 〔 Spacebar 〕.

3. Type the the location of the file you want to cancel (like this: *drive:\directory*).

4. Type the name of the file you want to cancel (like this: *filename.ext*).

5. Press 〔 Spacebar 〕 and type **/C**.

6. Press 〔↵Enter〕.

Why bother with names? To cancel all the print jobs, type **PRINT** **/T** and press ⏎Enter.

PROMPT

PROMPT casts a light into the DOS jungle of files and directories, by allowing you to customize the system prompt so you can see what you're doing as you change from directory to directory, looking for your missing files.

By default, the normal DOS prompt is a boring C>, which just sits there as you type one DOS command after another, waiting for you to do something else to entertain it. With the PROMPT command, you can make the DOS prompt *entertain you* by telling you such things as the current directory or drive, the current date, or the time.

Insert the PROMPT command in your AUTOEXEC.BAT for your DOS viewing pleasure; see the section, "Hacking Away at Files With the DOS Editor" later in this book for help.

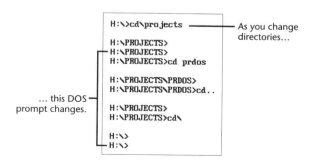

```
H:\>cd\projects                 ──── As you change
                                      directories...
H:\PROJECTS>
H:\PROJECTS>
H:\PROJECTS>cd prdos

H:\PROJECTS\PRDOS>
H:\PROJECTS\PRDOS>cd..

H:\PROJECTS>
H:\PROJECTS>cd\

H:\>
H:\>
```

... this DOS prompt changes.

Looking for the perfect prompt? See *The Complete Idiot's Guide to DOS*, Chapter 7, "Navigating the DOS Jungle of Files and Directories."

PROMPT: Displaying the Current Directory and Drive

This version of the PROMPT command wins the MISS POPULARITY award, hands down (in fact, you'll find this PROMPT command already in your AUTOEXEC.BAT, thanks to the DOS setup program):

1. Type **PROMPT**.

2. Press `Spacebar`.

3. Type **PG**

4. Press `⏎Enter`.

The resulting prompt looks like this:

```
C:\WORD\PROJECTS>
```

which displays the current drive (C:) and directory (\WORD\PROJECTS).

PROMPT: Displaying the Time in Your Prompt

This version displays the time along with the ever-popular current drive and directory:

1. Type **PROMPT**.

2. Press `Spacebar`.

3. Type **$T** and press `Spacebar`.

If you don't own a calendar, or if you often pull all-nighters to get important reports done at the last minute, you can include the current date too. Type **$D**.

4. Type **PG**.

5. Press **⏎Enter**.

Here's the result (DOS speaks in military time):

```
14:30:02.59 C:\WORD\PROJECTS>
```

Of course, the prompt is only updated when you press Enter, so it can display the wrong time for quite awhile, until you press Enter again.

To knock off some of this nonsense, type

PROMPT THHHHH$H PG

and you'll have a shorter time:

```
14:30  C:\WORD\PROJECTS>
```

The $H deletes one character from the previous parameter (in this case, the time). Using six of them causes the fractional parts of a second to be erased from the regular time display.

PROMPT: Adding a Message to the Prompt

You can add your own secret message to your prompt like this:

1. Type **PROMPT**.

2. Press **Spacebar**.

3. Type your message.

4. Type **$G**.

5. Press (↵Enter).

Here's what mine looks like (obviously, yours will vary depending on your message):

```
Enter a command, why don't ya?>
```

PROMPT: Creating a Two-Line Prompt

When one line just isn't enough, PROMPT lets you create several lines. All you have to do is insert the symbol for a carriage return in your prompt: **$_**. Follow these steps:

1. Type **PROMPT**.

2. Press (⎵Spacebar).

3. Type your message.

4. Type **$_** (dollar sign and underscore).

5. **(Optional)** For a three-line prompt, type another message and repeat step 4.

6. Type **PG**.

7. Press (↵Enter).

This is the sort of prompt you might get for your trouble:

```
Enter a command, why don't ya?
C:\>
```

As you type DOS commands, they appear on the second line, after the greater than sign.

RAMDRIVE.SYS

RAMDRIVE.SYS creates a disk drive out of thin air (actually, it creates it out of memory), making for a very fast disk drive. Beware, however: the RAM drive disappears when you turn off the computer, along with all the data you put on it, so RAM drives are not practical for most everyday uses.

Another warning: creating a RAM disk is okay if your PC has lots of RAM (like over 8MB). Otherwise, don't bother, 'cause you'll take away the stuff your programs need the most (RAM) to create something they may not be able to use (a RAM disk).

You load RAMDRIVE.SYS through your CONFIG.SYS, so get your tool kit and jump over to the section, "Hacking Away at Files With the DOS Editor" later in this book.

In a line in your CONFIG.SYS:

1. Type `DEVICE=C:\DOS\RAMDRIVE.SYS`.

2. Press (Spacebar) and type the size of the RAM disk in bytes.

For example, to create a smallish RAM disk that's 2MB (2,048 bytes), type:

```
DEVICE=C:\DOS\RAMDRIVE.SYS 2048
```

3. Press (Spacebar).

4. Type one of the following:

/**A** (to create the RAM disk out of expanded memory)

/**E** (to create the RAM disk out of extended memory).

5. Press ⏎Enter.

> DOS, picky as it is, will need you to provide access to either expanded memory (via EMM386.SYS) or extended memory (via HIMEM.SYS) by including the proper commands in the CONFIG.SYS *before* you do the RAMDRIVE thing.

Your baby RAM disk is assigned the next available drive letter, which is usually D:. You can then copy program files to D: to make the programs run faster. For example, you could copy your spelling dictionary to the RAM disk, and use it to speed up a spell check. Or copy your file compression program (such as PKUNZIP) to the RAM disk, and use it to unzip your compressed files. Make sure you save your data files to a real drive (such as C:) before you turn off your PC, 'cause everything on the fake drive D: is erased when you power down.

If you use Windows, change the setting for your temp directory to the RAM disk, to make printing in Windows super-fast (at least for Windows). In your AUTOEXEC.BAT, add something like:

```
MD D:\TEMP
SET TEMP=D:\TEMP
```

RD (RMDIR)

RD removes unslightly warts and unwanted directories the old-fashioned way—after they are empty. You must delete all the files in a directory yourself before you can remove it with RD.

If this is way too bogus for you, remove your directories the modern way, with DELTREE.

To remove a directory, you delete its files with the DEL command, then you use the RD command to get rid of it:

1. Type **CD**\.

2. Type the name of the directory you want to delete.

3. Press ⏎Enter.

4. Type **DEL** ***.*** and press ⏎Enter.

5. Type **CD..** and press ⏎Enter.

6. Type **RD** and press ⎵Spacebar.

7. Type the name of the directory you want to delete.

8. Press ⏎Enter.

Try This!

For example, to remove the C:\DATA directory, change to that directory (**CD****DATA**) and delete its contents (**DEL** ***.***). Then change to the directory above \DATA (**CD..**) and remove it (**RD** **DATA**).

Got lots of pesky directories to remove? Get yourself a can of Raid, and check out *The Complete Idiot's Guide to DOS*, Chapter 13, "Let Your Fingers Do the Walking— Directory Assistance."

REM

Play the critic and use REM to add comments to your batch files. They won't be seen when your batch file is running, but they're fun anyway. For example, you could add comments to yourself, explaining what your batch file does. This will make it easier to make changes when your user comes back and says, "It's great, but can we make one little change . . . ?" You can also use this handy-dandy command to disable certain lines in your CONFIG.SYS temporarily without deleting them.

For info on a glamorous career in editing files, see the section, "Hacking Away at Files With the DOS Editor" later in this book.

In a batch file (such as AUTOEXEC.BAT):

1. Type **REM**.

2. Press [Spacebar].

3. Type your comment.

For example, type:

    REM This command does something I'm sure.

You can also insert the command REM in front of existing commands in your CONFIG.SYS, to put them on temporary hiatus:

    REM DEVICE=C:\DOS\BOGUS.SYS

REN (RENAME)

A file by any other name will still spell as sweet, but that doesn't mean you have to live with a dorky filename like: DUH.DOC. Rename the file with the REN command to something that makes sense, like: POORSALE.DOC.

1. Change to the directory of the file you want to rename (like this: **CD***directory*). Press ⏎Enter.

2. Type **REN**.

3. Press ⎵Spacebar⎵.

4. Type the old filename.

5. Press ⎵Spacebar⎵.

6. Type the new filename.

7. Press ⏎Enter.

Try This!

For example, to rename MYFILE.DOC to HANDSOFF.DOC, type **REN MYFILE.DOC HANDSOFF.DOC**.

Want to know what's in a (re)name? See *The Complete Idiot's Guide to DOS*, Chapter 11, "Standing at the Copier, Copying Files."

REPLACE

REPLACE is a copy-like command for snobbish users only. With REPLACE, you can copy "selected" files, replacing only the files you need to.

Try This!

For example, why copy all those worksheet files from Johnny's Lotus diskette, when you may already have newer versions on your hard disk? With REPLACE, you can copy only the files you don't have, or files that are newer.

1. Type **REPLACE**.

2. Press ⎵Spacebar⎵.

3. Type the the location of the files you want to copy (like this: ***drive*:*directory***).

4. Type the name(s) of the file(s) you want to copy.

To copy more than one file at a time, get wild with a wildcard. For example, to copy all the files from a diskette that end in .WK4, type **A:*.WK4**.

5. Press [Spacebar].

6. Type the location of the files you want to replace (like this: ***drive*:*directory***).

For example, to copy all those worksheet files onto your hard disk and replace any files in the \\PROJECTS directory, type this:

REPLACE A:*.WK4 C:\\PROJECTS

7. **(Optional)** Add any of these optional switches. First, press [Spacebar], then type the switch as shown. Be sure to press [Spacebar] between each switch and the next one if you add more than one.

> To replace only old files type **/U**.

> To copy only files that you don't already have, type **/A**.

You can't use both the /U and the /A switch at the same time. Bummer. Choose one, then use the REPLACE command a second time and use the other:

REPLACE A:*.WK4 C:\\PROJECTS /A

REPLACE A:*.WK4 C:\\PROJECTS /U

To have REPLACE prompt you before it replaces a file, type /**P**.

To replace files in subdirectories too, type /**S**.

8. Press ⏎Enter.

RESTORE

Oops, you've come to the wrong place. To restore files from a backup, see the versatile MSBACKUP command. It slices, it dices, and it restores your files too.

The RESTORE command is still included with DOS 6.2, even though you probably will never use it, unless you have to restore files from a very old backup which was done with the BACKUP command, and not with MSBACKUP.

Stuck trying to restore some old files? See *The Complete Idiot's Guide to DOS*, Chapter 15, "Restoring Your Hard Disk."

SCANDISK

SCANDISK helps the Felix in you get over the Oscar in DOS. You see, DOS is downright sloppy when it deletes files. As a result, you probably have little parts of old deleted files sitting around in your DOS junkyard, trading stories and hubcaps. These parts of old files that were never deleted are called *lost clusters* or *lost chains*. Run SCANDISK from time to time to get rid of these old file parts and free up otherwise-unused disk space.

1. Exit all programs, including Windows and the DOS Shell.

2. Type **SCANDISK**.

3. Press ⟨ Spacebar ⟩.

4. Type the letter of the drive you want to clean up (with a colon after it, like this: *drive:*).

For example, type **SCANDISK C:** to clean up the mess on your main hard drive. By the way, you can't use SCANDISK on a network drive, or a CD-ROM.

5. If DOS finds a problem, opt to fix it.

For example, you may encounter the following:

ScanDisk found 128 bytes of data on drive C that might be one or more lost files or directories, but which is probably just taking up space.

If you think ScanDisk's uncovered some long-lost data, click on **Save** to save it in a file. Normally, you'll click on **Delete** since SCANDISK usually finds data from some old deleted file you don't even need anymore.

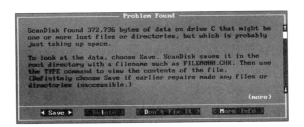

6. (**Optional**) If you're asked to create an Undo diskette, stick one in a diskette drive and click on either **Drive A** or **Drive B**. If you don't want to create one, click on **Skip Undo**.

An *Undo diskette* allows you to change your mind and undo what ScanDisk does. But take it from me, Undo diskettes are risky, like jumping off a tightrope in hopes there's a net below. I always skip it.

7. **(Optional)** ScanDisk can also check out your hard disk for physical problems with a surface scan. Click on **Yes** to start it, or **No** to bypass this step.

Surface scans take a while, and rarely turn up any problems, so don't feel that you have to do one every single time. Once a month or so is plenty, unless you are getting errors like `Sector not found reading drive C:` or `Data error reading drive C:`. The process is a bit noisy, so if you decide to do it, get out your earplugs before you start the scan.

8. **(Optional)** After the scan is complete, you can view a log of the results by clicking on **View Log**.

9. Click on **Exit** when you're through.

For more info on ScanDisk, scan these pages of *The Complete Idiot's Guide to DOS*, Chapter 5, "Becoming a Disk Jockey."

SET

Sometimes DOS or programs need to write things down in order to remember them. For example, DOS writes a note to itself at startup, telling itself where it left its most important part: COMMAND.COM. (That's one note you don't want to lose!) The place where these notes are kept is called the environment area. You can add notes yourself with the SET command. Programs or DOS can then check the environment area to find out which settings you prefer in a given situation.

The SET command is often placed in the AUTOEXEC.BAT as a permanent fixture. To learn the fascinating art of editing files, see "Hacking Away at Files With the DOS Editor" later in this book.

Somewhere in your AUTOEXEC.BAT file,

1. Type **SET**.

2. Press [Spacebar].

3. Type the name of the variable you want to set.

4. Type **=**.

5. Type the value to which you want to set the variable.

For example, type **SET TEMP=C:\WINDOWS\TEMP**.

For more info on SET, see *The Complete Idiot's Guide to DOS*, Chapter 17, "AUTOEXEC.BAT, CONFIG.SYS, and Other Secret Code Words".

SET: Viewing the Contents of the Environment Area

At a DOS prompt,

1. Type **SET**.

2. Press [↵Enter].

```
H:\>set
COMSPEC=C:\DOS622\COMMAND.COM
PROMPT=$p$g
PATH=C:\DOS;C:\WINDOWS;C:\BIN\WORD;H:\NC;H:\COLLAGE\DOS
TEMP=C:\WINDOWS\TEMP
PCPLUS=C:\PCPLUS

H:\>
```

What you might see when you use the SET command.

The DOS commands PATH, PROMPT, SHELL, DIRCMD, and COPYCMD all leave notes in the environment area about the settings you've chosen (without using the SET command). If a program wants you to use the SET command to change any of its settings, it'll tell you so in its user manual.

SETVER

SETVER is used to fool old programs into thinking you're running an older version of DOS, so that when they run under DOS 6.2 they won't choke and die.

If you've accidentally turned to this page looking for another command, don't stop too long. Potentially geeky stuff ahead.

Courtesy of the DOS Setup program, you've already got the SETVER device driver loaded in your CONFIG.SYS:

```
DEVICE=C:\DOS\SETVER.EXE
```

This command loads the version table, a listing of out-of-date programs and the DOS version you have to fool them into thinking you're running. *Don't mess with this command or remove it.* It's basically harmless, but you need it if you're going to use the SETVER command that's coming up.

SETVER: Viewing the Version Table

To view the real exciting version table, do this from the DOS prompt:

1. Type **SETVER**.

2. Press ⌷ Spacebar ⌷.

3. Type ¦ **More**.

4. Press ⏎Enter⏎.

SETVER: Adding a Program to the Version Table

To add an out-of-date program to the version table:

Adding a program to the version table is no guaranteee that it'll be fooled by your little scheme. If the program is truly incompatible with DOS 6.2, this little scheme won't get it to run correctly. Contact the manufacturer for an update.

1. Type **SETVER**.

2. Press [Spacebar].

3. Type the program's filename.

4. Press [Spacebar].

5. Type the DOS version it needs to believe you're running instead of DOS 6.2.

6. Press [↵Enter].

For example, type **SETVER OLDPRGRM.EXE 3.30**

Well, you've gone and done it. Restart your system for the changes to take effect.

SHARE

SHARE forces DOS to share, instead of hogging all the files. This command is required by Windows, network programs, and other multitasking programs. These programs need SHARE to enable file sharing (allowing multiple programs to use the same file) and record locking (preventing multiple people from using the same file while changes are being made to it).

If you have Windows installed, or if you're on a network, you already have this command in your AUTOEXEC.BAT. Pass Go and collect your $200 (then send me the name of the person who gave you the cash).

If you're dying to know the secrets of editing your AUTOEXEC.BAT (and who isn't?) see the section, "Hacking Away at Files With the DOS Editor" later in this book.

In your AUTOEXEC.BAT:

1. Type **SHARE**.

2. (Optional) To set the maximum amount of memory space (in bytes) for all this sharing nonsense, press ⌗ Spacebar ⌗ and type **/F:space**. (The default is 2048.)

3. (Optional) To set the maximum number of file/record locks, press ⌗ Spacebar ⌗ and type **/L:numlocks**. (The default is 20.)

SHELL

SHELL tells DOS which command interpreter's in use, and where it's being kept. You can use this command to load some other command interpreter (yeah, right—as if you'd ever want to do that. I'll just stay with good old trustworthy COMMAND.COM, thank you very much).

Compliments of the MS-DOS Setup program, this command is already in your CONFIG.SYS, to point to the directory where DOS resides. *Don't mess with this command.* DOS could lose itself (and you won't be able to start your computer) if you do.

Editing the CONFIG.SYS is tricky stuff (of course, so is messing around with the SHELL command, so why get scared now?) See the section, "Hacking Away at Files With the DOS Editor" later in this book.

OK, it's not as if I didn't warn you. If you insist on using this command, in your CONFIG.SYS:

1. Type **SHELL=**.

2. Type the location of command processor you want to use (like this: *drive:\directory*).

3. Type the name of the command processor.

4. Press ⌊ Spacebar ⌋ and type whatever additional switches the new command interpreter requires.

For example, to load COMMAND.COM (the DOS command interpreter) into memory and keep it there (a good idea, by my way of thinking) add the /P switch:

```
SHELL=C:\DOS\COMMAND.COM C:\DOS /P
```

The directory (C:\DOS) is included as a parameter because DOS uses it to remember where the COMMAND.COM file is kept. Your alternate command interpreter may not require either this directory specification or a /P switch. Check its manual for details. COMMAND.COM also uses a /E switch, which you might find helpful. See the next section for details.

For more info on SHELL, see *The Complete Idiot's Guide to DOS*, Chapter 17, "AUTOEXEC.BAT, CONFIG.SYS, and Other Secret Code Words."

SHELL: Enlarging the Environment Area

OK, there is one good reason to use the SHELL command, and that's to enlarge the environment area, a place in memory where DOS and some other programs keep important information they don't want to forget.

> ## Tip
>
> If you see the message, "Out of environment space" use this command. You might see this if your PATH command is too fat, you've got a big PROMPT, or you use a lot of SET commands in your AUTOEXEC.BAT.

In your CONFIG.SYS:

1. Type **SHELL=C:\DOS\COMMAND.COM**.

2. Press [Spacebar] and type **C:\DOS**.

3. Press [Spacebar] and specify the amount of memory (in bytes) you want set aside for the environment area (like this: **/E:*nnnn***).

> ## Try This!
>
> The default is a measly 256. This number needs to be a multiple of 16, and it can't be larger than 32768. Don't make it too big, or you'll waste RAM.

4. Press [Spacebar] and type **/P**.

The /P switch makes the COMMAND.COM file permanent, which means it's not going anywhere until you reboot, which is a mighty good thing indeed, 'cause without it, your PC makes a good paperweight (but that's about all). Temporary DOS prompts are not loaded permanently, which means you type **EXIT** to get out of them. See EXIT for more details.

SMARTDRV (SMARTDrive)

SMARTDrive makes your hard disk faster by making it smarter. How it works is unimportant; all you've got to do is install SMARTDrive once, then forget it.

All right, if you have to know, SMARTDrive creates a cache in memory which acts as a "holding tank" for data read from the hard disk. The next time that data is needed, the PC gets it from memory, which is quicker because RAM is faster than the hard disk. As the disk cache gets full of recent data, the least-requested information is overwritten, ensuring that the cache stays full of often-requested data.

SMARTDrive also caches data being written to the hard disk (for example, when you save a file). Instead of stopping every few seconds to write one thing or the other, SMARTDrive holds onto multiple requests to save data until the write cache gets full. Then it's all written to the hard disk in one step.

SMARTDrive is installed through the AUTOEXEC.BAT. For a lesson in editing etiquette, see the section, "Hacking Away at Files With the DOS Editor" later in this book.

Both DOS and Windows install SMARTDrive for you automatically, so you probably won't have any need to do this. But if you feel like it anyway, in your AUTOEXEC.BAT:

1. Type `C:\DOS\SMARTDRV.EXE`.

2. **(Optional)** To disable caching on your CD-ROM, press ⌷ Spacebar ⌷ and type `/U`.

SMARTDrive loads into extended memory, so it would be nice if you had some available. Be sure you have this command in your CONFIG.SYS:

```
DEVICE=C:\DOS\HIMEM.SYS
```

Having it prevents SMARTDrive from slamming into a memory wall.

Want to get smarter about SMARTDrive? Check out *The Complete Idiot's Guide to DOS*, Chapter 5, "Becoming a Disk Jockey."

SMARTDRV: Clearing the Cache Before Powering Down

Before you send your PC off to sleep, it's a *very good idea* to clear the cache, forcing it to let loose of your last bits of data and save them onto the hard disk.

At the DOS prompt:

1. Type **SMARTDRV**.
2. Press ⸢ Spacebar ⸥.
3. Type /**C**.
4. Press ⸢↵Enter⸥.

STACKS

The STACKS command helps DOS track interrupts. Interrupts are sent by the PC's various hardware components (keyboard, mouse, disk drives, etc.) in an attempt to get the CPU's attention. For example, when you press a key or click a mouse button, an interrupt is sent to tell the CPU to stop what it's doing and pay attention to the keyboard or the mouse.

If your STACKS command doesn't allow for enough interrupts, your PC can go into overload, running around like a chicken with its head cut off, screaming, "Stack Overflow! Stack Overflow!" The solution of course, is to increase the number of stacks.

You've gotta put this command in your CONFIG.SYS to make it work (some commands are so picky). For a lesson in editing, turn to the section, "Hacking Away at Files With the DOS Editor" later in this book. For a lesson in stupidity, try bungee-jumping.

On a blank line in your CONFIG.SYS file:

1. Type **STACKS=**.

2. Type the number of stacks desired.

3. Type a comma (**,**).

4. Type the desired stack size.

5. Press ⏎Enter.

For example, try this command: **STACKS=9,256**.

But because I use Windows, I use the command STACKS=0,0 instead, which saves some RAM and lets Windows fend for itself in its own Windows way (Got this tip from a book on memory management, and I've never had a problem with this setting and running Windows, but if your Windows programs begin to flake out, change it back to 9,258). Full disclaimer of responsibility; STACKS=0,0 void where prohibited.

For more info on STACKS, see *The Complete Idiot's Guide to DOS*, Chapter 17, "AUTOEXEC.BAT, CONFIG.SYS, and Other Secret Code Words."

SUBMENU

SUBMENU adds a menu below a menu on your startup menu, making it down right difficult to write this sentence without the word "menu." With SUBMENU, you can hide the menu choice for the game "Blonde Showgirls From Venus" where your boss will never find it and learn why your production report is three months late.

For more menu midnight madness, check out the commands: INCLUDE, MENUCOLOR, MENUDEFAULT, and MENUITEM, and see the section "More Than You'll Want to Know About Configuring Your PC," later in this book.

Somewhere near the beginning of your CONFIG.SYS file, insert these commands:

1. Type **SUBMENU=**.

2. Type a label for this menu selection.

For example, type **SUBMENU=NETWK**.

3. **(Optional)** Type a comma (**,**) followed by a description of this menu item.

Suppose you want to set up a menu system which gives the user a choice between basic configuration (for everyday duties) and network configuration (for connecting to the company network system and causing havoc). On the network menu, you want to offer two (count 'em, two) choices. Type this:

```
[MENU]
MENUITEM=BASIC, Basic Configuration
SUBMENU=NETWRK, Network Configurations
```

Later in the CONFIG.SYS, you define the two choices for the submenu by including the label [NETWRK] and its two commands. For example:

```
[NETWRK]
MENUITEM=ACCTG, Accounting Network
MENUITEM=CSR, Client Services Network
```

Still later at the CONFIG.SYS corral, you include the labels [**ACCTG**] and [**CSR**], each followed by a series of commands you want carried out when those selections are chosen from your submenu. Better do something for [**BASIC**] too, or it'll be pretty boring if someone chooses that selection.

SUBST

In a bit of DOS weirdness, SUBST makes a directory appear to be a drive by assigning it its own letter. For example, drive Q: could really be Secret Agent Directory \BOND. Then when you copy files to Q: they end up in the \BOND directory. You could also delete, move, or rename files this way, along with other fascinating shortcuts.

SUBST is a very bad command to party with. He hardly gets along with anyone, arguing loudly with ASSIGN, DEFRAG, DISKCOPY, DISKCOMP, FASTOPEN, FDISK, FORMAT, LABEL, SYS, and UNDELETE. He also doesn't party well with Windows.

1. Type **SUBST**.

2. Press ⌈ Spacebar ⌉.

3. Type the drive letter to be assigned to the directory.

4. Press ⌈ Spacebar ⌉.

5. Type the drive and directory you want to substitute (like this: ***drive:\directory***).

6. Press ⌈↵Enter⌉.

For example, to substitute the letter J: for the directory
C:\PROJECTS\PRDOS\ORIG, type:

SUBST J: C:\PROJECT\PRDOS\ORIG

After your fingers have gotten the rest they deserve after
typing a command like that, type just **J:** anytime you
want to access C:\PROJECTS\PRDOS\ORIG. Your fingers
will thank you.

In order to assign a drive letter to a directory with
SUBST, you're gonna need the LASTDRIVE command
in your CONFIG.SYS:

LASTDRIVE=J

or whatever letter you decide to use for your directory. You may already have this command in your
CONFIG.SYS, if you use DriveSpace. Just change the
letter as necessary.

SUBST: To Display the Current Drive Aliases

1. Type **SUBST**.
2. Press ⏎Enter.

SUBST: To Remove a Directory Substitution

1. Type **SUBST**.
2. Type the drive letter be assigned to the directory
   (like this: *drive:*).
3. Press ⎵ Spacebar.
4. Type **/D**.
5. Press ⏎Enter.

Try This!

For example, to return to the bad old days of long directory names, type this:

SUBST J: /D

SYS

In case of emergency, break glass. In case of a PC emergency, have a diskette handy that you can boot (start) your PC from. To create a bootable diskette, format it with the /S switch. If you don't want to go to all that trouble, copy the system files onto a diskette with the SYS command.

1. Type **SYS**.

2. Press [Spacebar].

3. Type the drive letter to which you want to copy the system files (like this: ***drive:***).

4. Press [↵Enter].

Try This!

For example, type **SYS A:**. The four files, IO.SYS, MSDOS.SYS, COMMAND.COM, and (if you have a compressed drive) DRVSPACE.BIN will be copied to the diskette. Don't expect to see them though— they're hiding. All except COMMAND.COM, which was never good at playing games as a child.

TIME

Does anybody know what time it is? Does anybody really care? If you do and you've lost your watch, you can use the TIME command to find out.

1. Type **TIME**.

2. Press ⏎Enter. The time is displayed.

3. Press ⏎Enter.

Just can't get enough about the TIME command? Well, see *The Complete Idiot's Guide to DOS*, Chapter 3, "Gentlemen (and Ladies) Start Your PCs!"

TIME: Changing the Time

1. Type **TIME**.

2. Press ⏎Enter.

3. Enter a new time (like this: *hh:mm*).

4. Press ⏎Enter.

DOS marches to a military clock, so to enter 2:30 p.m., type **14:30**, Sir!

TREE

In the infinite wisdom of accounting departments everywhere, yours has decided to save a few bucks and replace your old clunker PC with Tom's old clunker PC. (Tom, with two days seniority over you, gets a new PC—and a bash on the head the next time you see him.) Use the TREE command to display a listing of all the directories Tom has set up on his PC, so you can see what you're playing with now.

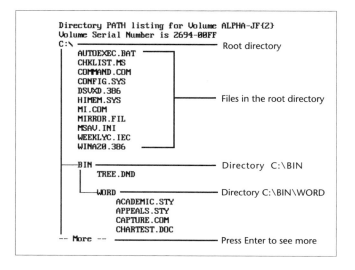

1. Type **TREE**.

2. **(Optional)** Press !!Spacebar!! and specify the drive to view if it isn't already the active drive (like this: ***drive*:**).

3. Type the directory you want the listing to start with (like this: ***directory***).

Try This!

To start at the root directory and list all subdirectories, just type a little \\ (backslash).

4. **(Optional)** To show files in addition to directories, press ⌈ Spacebar ⌉ and type **/F**.

5. Press ⌈ Spacebar ⌉ and type ¦ **MORE**.

MORE's a handy fellow who slows down the display for commands too lazy to do it themselves. After one screenful of directories is displayed, you'll see:

— More —

Press ⏎Enter to continue.

6. Press ⏎Enter.

Branch out to new vistas with the TREE command. See *The Complete Idiot's Guide to DOS*, Chapter 10, "Lost Something? How to Find Files With the DIR Command." Now with 50% more puns.

TREE: Printing the Listing

Printing the listing is easier than looking at it on-screen, where you could easily strain something important like your brain, trying to memorize about 100 directories as you scroll through the list.

1. Type **TREE**.

2. (Optional) Press [Spacebar] and specify the drive to view if it isn't already the active drive: (like this: *drive:*).

3. (Optional) Unless you want to start the listing with the current directory, type the directory you want the listing to start with (like this: *\directory*).

4. (Optional) To show files in addition to directories, press [Spacebar] and type /**F**.

5. Press [Spacebar] and type /**A**.

The /A switch sends the data to your printer in a non-graphical, printer-friendly way.

6. Press [Spacebar] and type **>PRN**.

For example, to print a listing of all the directories and files on your PC's hard drive, type a command that's almost as long as the listing itself:

TREE C:\ /F /A >PRN

7. Press [↵Enter].

TYPE

TYPE displays the contents of a file on-screen in brilliant DOS-O-Vision. As an added feature, if the file you're looking at is a program file (one that ends in .EXE or .COM), you'll meet a whole gang of wacky characters as your PC beeps constantly, alerting everyone in the building to the fact that you just tried to use TYPE on a file that can't be displayed. You'll get this same reaction when you use TYPE on files created in programs such as 1-2-3, Word, WordPerfect, etc.

The TYPE command is perfectly civilized when used on simple text files such as your CONFIG.SYS, AUTOEXEC.BAT, or files that say irresistably: README.TXT.

1. Type **TYPE**.

2. Press [Spacebar].

3. Type the file location (like this:
   drive*:*directory).

4. Type the name of the file you want to view.

5. Press [Spacebar] and type ¦ **MORE**.

6. Press [↵Enter].

Text

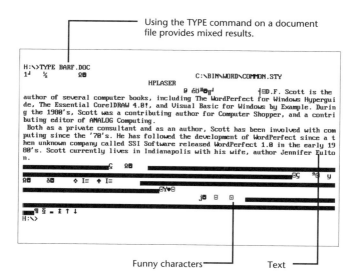

Using the TYPE command on a document
file provides mixed results.

Funny characters ——— Text ———

While it's advisable not to view the contents of
most snack foods, viewing text files is OK. For
example, to see the contents of a file called
README.TXT so you can learn the hidden
secrets on how to install that darn (sorry this
book is rated PG) program that you've been
trying to install for three darn days, type:

TYPE C:\DARNPRGM\README.TXT ¦ MORE

UNDELETE (DOS Version)

If you delete the wrong file accidentally, what should you do? Well, if you have a version of the file on a diskette, you can copy it back onto your hard disk. But what do you do if you don't have a recent copy of the file, and you're out of tissues? Just use the UNDELETE command to try to recover your dignity and as many files as possible.

> Tip of the Week: You'll have the best luck getting your files back if you don't do anything else (I MEAN NOTHING) on your PC until you've recovered your files.

> If you have Windows, there's no need to dirty your hands with DOS. Windows comes with a version of UNDELETE designed just for mouse pushers. See "UNDELETE (Windows)."

Want the full story? Check out *The Complete Idiot's Guide to DOS*, Chapter 12, "Spring Cleaning—Deleting Unwanted Files."

UNDELETE (DOS): Increasing Your Chances of Getting Your Files Back

Want to avoid sorting all those unlabeled diskettes you own, in quest of the only existing copy of that file you accidentally deleted? You can. Use either Delete Senty or Delete Tracker. Interested? I thought you might be.

How does this work? Well, when a file's deleted, it's not really removed. But forgetful DOS may or may not remember where it stored all the pieces of the file. Delete Tracker and Delete Sentry, acting as responsible parents keep track of the exact location of each piece of a file (along with their socks, car keys, and wallets) and provide the missing information to DOS. Delete Tracker uses less hard disk space to track deleted files, but it doesn't do as good a job as Delete Sentry, so choose your best weapon. (If you've got an itchy trigger finger, use Delete Sentry.)

To install Delete Tracker so you can sleep at night, place this command in your AUTOEXEC.BAT:

1. Type **UNDELETE**.

2. Press [Spacebar].

3. Type the letter of the drive whose files you want to track (like this: /**T*drive***).

For example, type this:

UNDELETE /TC

If you have more than one drive, add that one for good measure:

UNDELETE /TC /TD

To install Delete Sentry so you can sleep at night, during the day, through a thunderstorm, a hurricane, flash flood, or famine, place this command in your AUTOEXEC.BAT:

1. Type **UNDELETE**.

2. Press [Spacebar].

3. Type the letter of the drive whose files you want to track (like this: /**S*drive***).

For example, type this:

UNDELETE /SC

If you have more than one drive, add that one for sleepful nights without Sominex:

UNDELETE /SC /SD

UNDELETE (DOS): Listing Recently Deleted Files

To see a list of files deleted from the current directory that you might be able to bring back from the edge of destruction:

1. Type **UNDELETE**.

2. Press [Spacebar].

3. Type /**LIST**.

4. Press [↵Enter].

```
Copyright (C) 1987-1993 Central Point Software, Inc.
All rights reserved.

Directory: H:\PROJECTS\PRDOS
File Specifications: *.*

    Delete Sentry control file not found.

    Deletion-tracking file not found.

    MS-DOS directory contains   3 deleted files.
    Of those,   2 files may be recovered.

Using the MS-DOS directory method.

      ?-Z     BAK    51200  8-04-94 11:01a  ...A
      ?WRL1173 TMP   15872  7-25-94  4:35p  ...A
   ** ?0FIG01 PCX    24109  6-15-94 12:40p  ...A ──┐

   "**" indicates the first cluster of the file
        is unavailable and cannot be recovered
        with the UNDELETE command.

H:\PROJECTS\PRDOS>
```

Can't undelete this file

Use the UNDELETE command on any of the files you
see listed. Sorry, but Mr. Hangman says you can't
undelete files with the mark of death (**).

UNDELETE (DOS): Undeleting a File

So you were clever and decided to delete last month's
figures from your hard disk. At that moment, your boss
walked in and asked you to do a comparison between
this month's sales and last month's. To save the file and
your job, change to the directory in which the file was
last seen, then:

1. Type **UNDELETE**.

2. Press [Spacebar].

3. Type the filename.

For example, type this very quickly (before the boss
comes back):

   UNDELETE   APRSALES.WK4

4. Press [⏎Enter].

You might be asked to supply the first letter of the
filename, as in

      ?PRSALES.WK4
      Please supply the missing letter:

Enter the missing letter (in this case, the letter **A**) and
press [⏎Enter]. If you don't really know what the missing
letter is, it's OK, because neither does DOS. So type
anything.

UNDELETE (DOS): Undeleting Several Files at Once

To recover all files that can be recovered in the current directory:

1. Type **UNDELETE**.

2. Press ⎡ Spacebar ⎤.

3. Type **/ALL**.

4. Press ⎡↵Enter⎤.

You can undelete selected files instead of all of them by using wildcards, such as:

```
UNDELETE C:\DUMB\*.DOC
```

For a wild review, check out the section, "The Least You Need to Know About DOS" at the front of this book. You know, it's that part you originally skipped, but which is becoming painfully clear was placed there for a really good reason. (Honestly. You slave all day over a hot keyboard . . .)

UNDELETE (Windows Version)

Undeleting is probably the most fun I have in Windows (other than playing with my screen saver). It gives me such power, knowing I can act like an idiot and delete any file I want, then say "Oops" and get it back.

You'll have the best luck getting your files back if you don't do anything else (I MEAN NOTHING) on your PC until you've recovered them. (Here's an idea if you desperately need a vacation: just delete some files and tell your boss, "But the book says not to do nothin'!")

Deleting the directory that your files were in usually means you won't be able to get them back. So don't delete a directory until you're sure you want to say a permanent goodbye.

Wait, there's more! Check out *The Complete Idiot's Guide to DOS*, Chapter 12, "Spring Cleaning—Deleting Unwanted Files".

UNDELETE (Windows): Starting Undelete

Undelete for Windows, unlike Jimmy Hoffa, is easy to locate:

1. Double-click on the **Microsoft Tools** program group to open it ▨.

2. Double-click on the **Undelete** icon ▨.

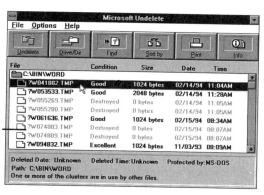

Files that you can't undelete are grayed.

If a file's grayed out so you can't select it, that means it's trashed, at least as far as Windows Undelete is concerned. However, for a reason known only to DOS, you might still be able to retrieve the file if you leave mouseland and head for the DOS prompt. From there, try using Undelete for DOS to raise the file from the dead. You might have better luck than you did with Windows Undelete.

UNDELETE (Windows): Starting Undelete From File Manager

1. Click on a directory in which you want to undelete a file.

2. Click on **File**.

3. Click on **Undelete**.

UNDELETE (Windows): Increasing Your Chances of Getting Your Files Back

If you don't undelete a file right after accidentally deleting it, you may not be able to get that file back. Sorry. But if you act now, with this one time offer you can greatly increase your chances of not sorting through every diskette you own in a vain attempt to find the only existing copy of that file you accidentally deleted. Use either Delete Senty or Delete Tracker. Interested? I thought you might be.

Delete Tracker uses less disk space than Delete Sentry to track deleted files, but it's not as good a protection as Super Duper Delete Sentry, now with MSD. For the full story on these two, check out this same section under UNDELETE (DOS).

To install Delete Sentry or Delete Tracker so you can sleep at night, during the day, through a thunderstorm, a hurricane, flash flood, or famine, follow these steps:

1. Start Windows Undelete.

2. Click on **Options**.

3. Click on **Configure Delete Protection**.

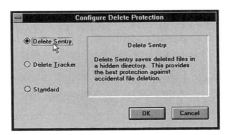

4. Click on **Delete Sentry** or **Delete Tracker**.

5. Click on **OK**.

6. (**Optional**) If you selected Delete Sentry, you can change any of the options you see here. Then click on **Drives**.

7. Click on the drives you want to protect.

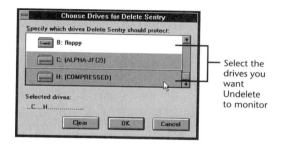

Select the drives you want Undelete to monitor

8. Click on **OK**.

9. (**Optional**) If you selected Delete Sentry, you're back at the Configure Delete Sentry dialog box. Click on **OK** again.

10. To make these changes permanent, click on **Save Changes To C:\Autoexec.Bat** and click on **OK**.

11. Exit Windows and reboot your PC for immediate, 24-hour protection.

UNDELETE (Windows): Changing Directories or Drives

Before you can undelete a file, you've got to move into the same directory from which you sent it to an early grave.

1. Start Windows Undelete.

2. Click on **Drives/Dir**.

3. **(Optional)** To change to a different drive, scroll to the bottom of the **Directories:** list and double-click on a drive letter, such as -**B**-.

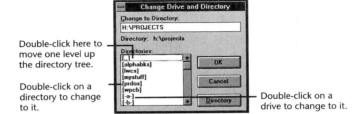

Double-click here to move one level up the directory tree.

Double-click on a directory to change to it.

Double-click on a drive to change to it.

4. Under **Directories:** double-click on a directory to change to it. Double-click on **..** to move one directory up in the DOS tree.

5. Click on **OK**.

UNDELETE (Windows): Undeleting a File

So you were clever and decided to delete last month's figures from your hard disk. At that moment, your boss walked in and asked you to do a comparison between this month's sales and last month's. To save the file and your job, change to the directory in which the file was last seen, then:

1. Click on the file you want to undelete. You can't undelete a file which is grayed (unavailable).

2. Click on **Undelete**.

You'll be asked to supply the first letter of the filename, as in:

```
Please type in the new first letter:
?PRSALES.WK4
```

Enter the missing letter (in this case, the letter **A**) and click on **OK**. If you don't really know what the missing letter is, it's OK, because neither does DOS. So type anything.

UNDELETE (Windows): Undeleting Several Files at Once

To recover all files that can be recovered in the current directory:

1. Click on **Options**.

2. Click on **Select By Name**.

3. Type in a wildcard specification.

For a wild review, check out the section, "The Least You Need to Know About DOS" at the front of this book.

4. Click on **OK**.

5. Click on **Undelete**.

6. Supply the missing letter for each file, and click on **OK**.

If the party's getting out of hand, send a few files home by clicking on **Options** and then **Unselect By Name**. Pick out the party crashers by typing in a wildcard combination to identify them, then click on **OK**.

UNFORMAT

UNFORMAT allows you to keep your job after the diskette you borrowed from your boss (and formatted) turns out to be the only copy of last year's budget reports. With UNFORMAT, you can undo your formatting job and recover the original data on the diskette.

This assumes however, that you didn't play "Russian roulette" with FORMAT and use the /U switch, which tells it to format the diskette so that you can't unformat it ever.

1. Type **UNFORMAT**.

2. Press [Spacebar].

3. Type the letter of the drive you want to restore.

4. Press [↵Enter].

For example, to unformat a disk in A:, type
UNFORMAT A:.

5. After the mirror image of the original diskette is found, you'll see a message asking you if you want to do this. Press [Y].

You might even get this to work, but only if you have not yet copied files onto the diskette you formatted by accident.

Got a lot of diskettes to fix? Check out *The Complete Idiot's Guide to DOS*, Chapter 6, "Diskette Disco."

VER

VER lets you know what DOS version your PC is using, in case you're planning to attend the next PC Geeks and Lonely Hearts Convention, or you're just one of those morbidly curious types.

1. Type **VER**.

2. Press ⏎Enter.

For the latest on the newest DOS versions, see *The Complete Idiot's Guide to DOS*, Chapter 9, "That's My Version and I'm Stickin' to It."

VERIFY

Allows you to slow your PC down to a crawl so that DOS can check to see whether what it thought it just saved was really saved after all. As an added feature, while your PC's tied up every time something is saved to disk, you can wonder why DOS would need a command like this in the first place. (Seriously, what VERIFY does is to double-check each write procedure, to make sure that DOS actually writes the file correctly, and not onto a bad spot on the disk.)

To really cripple your computer, put this command in your AUTOEXEC.BAT. Better yet, why not just take a vacation? After all, you're not going to get any work done while this command is in place.

VERIFY: Checking the Current VERIFY Status

1. Type **VERIFY**.

2. Press ⏎Enter.

VERIFY: Changing the VERIFY Status

1. Type **VERIFY**.

2. Press [Spacebar].

3. Type **ON** or **OFF**.

4. Press [↵Enter].

The folks at Microsoft might be loony for inventing a command like this, but you can approach write verification in a sane way and use the /V switch when you COPY important files, instead of using the VERIFY ON command to bring your computer tasks to a screaming halt.

VOL

Displays the label-label-label of the disk-disk-disk.

This command just shows you the electronic label that was placed there when you formatted the disk originally. To put a label there after formatting, or to change it, use the (of all things) LABEL command. Duh.

1. Type **VOL**.

2. Press [Spacebar].

3. Type the drive letter, followed by a colon (like this: *drive***:**).

4. Press [↵Enter].

VSAFE

Provides around the clock chemical-free virus protection. Using the MSAV command (see MS AntiVirus) only detects those viruses that are active at that time. To have ongoing protection, run VSafe, which runs in the background as you perform your normal computer tasks, then warns you of suspicious changes to your files.

The problem of using VSAFE is that it's way too anxious, going off more times than the neighbors' poodle that barks at passers-by, birds, bugs, and thin air. Frankly, I'd rather get a virus than use VSAFE. If you feel compelled to use VSAFE anyway (remember, I warned you), make sure you put it in your AUTOEXEC.BAT file so that it loads each day at startup.

Don't under any circumstances run VSAFE and then run Windows. In this scenario, don't put VSAFE in your AUTOEXEC.BAT; just type it at the DOS prompt. Then make sure you reboot after running VSAFE at the DOS prompt before you start Windows. Yech.

To start VSFAFE, follow these steps:

1. Type **VSAFE**.
2. Press ⏎Enter.

For more information on how to protect yourself and your files, see *The Complete Idiot's Guide to DOS*, Chapter 18, "Virus Got You Down?"

XCOPY

A four-star version of the COPY command, XCOPY copies entire directories and subdirectories (and their files) without drawing a breath.

1. Type **XCOPY**.
2. Press Spacebar.

3. Type the drive and directory to copy:

   ☞ To copy the entire disk, type ***drive*:**

   ☞ To copy a directory and its subdirectories, type drive:\directory.

4. Press [Spacebar].

5. Type the destination:

   ☞ To copy to the root directory of a disk: ***drive*:**

   ☞ To copy to a subdirectory: ***drive*:*directory**

6. Press [Spacebar].

7. Type **/S**.

8. **(Optional)** To copy empty directories too, press [Spacebar] and type **/E**.

9. Press [↵Enter].

For example, to copy all the files and subdirectories from A: to a directory on C: called \SUPERCPY, use
XCOPY A:\ C:\SUPERCPY /S.

Hacking Away at Files with the DOS Editor (EDIT.COM)

EDIT is kind of like a word processor, except it creates only plain text files, without fancy formatting such as bold or italics. EDIT comes free with DOS because the folks at Microsoft are part of a worldwide conspiracy of programmers everywhere to force humble human beings like us to "participate" in the computing experience by actually doing work, such as editing files.

With EDIT, the technicolor text editor, you can (if you're so inclined, and you can't talk some fool into doing it for you) make changes to any text file, or create some new tome. But EDIT is especially useful for changing system files, such as AUTOEXEC.BAT and CONFIG.SYS. (For more about these files, see the section "More Than You'll Want to Know About Configuring Your PC.")

To start the DOS Editor:

1. Type **EDIT**.

2. Press (⏎Enter).

3. Press (Esc) to clear the information box and to begin editing.

If you see the message **Can't find QBASIC.EXE**, then some techno toad has deleted a file you need to use EDIT. Find him and in real nice words, tell him to put it back. *Now*.

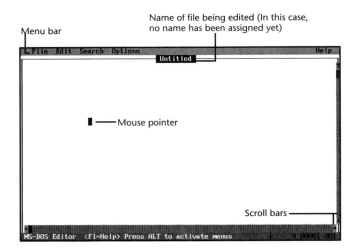

Name of file being edited (In this case, no name has been assigned yet)

Menu bar

Mouse pointer

Scroll bars

If EDIT has started successfully, then you're ready to start typing text if you're into creating a new file. To do as little work as possible (hey, that's my motto), open an *existing* file instead (such as AUTOEXEC.BAT), as described next.

EDIT: Opening a File to Edit

To read something such as a letter or a will, you open it. Once opened, you can make changes to it (such as leaving yourself the Wickley fortune). In a similar fashion, to edit a pre-existing file (such as AUTOEXEC.BAT or CONFIG.SYS), you must open it. You can then make changes and leave yourself a fortune in ancient DOS commands. What a treasure.

1. Start the DOS editor.

2. Click on **File**.

3. Click on **Open**.

Type the name of the file you
want to open, or use wildcards.

Double-click to get to
the root directory.

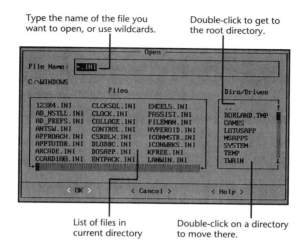

List of files in
current directory

Double-click on a directory
to move there.

4. **(Optional)** To open a file in a different directory,
   or on a different drive, double-click on it in the
   Dirs/Drives box.

To get to the root directory, where the
AUTOEXEC.BAT and CONFIG.SYS files are stored,
follow the breadcrumbs. More specifically, double-
click on the two dots **(..)** thingies at the top of the
Dirs/Drives list. (If you don't see these breadcrumbs,
you're already in the root directory!)

5. In the **File Name** box, type the name of the file
   you want to open.

You can get really wild and list files using wildcards.
Just type a wildcard combination and press ⏎Enter
to see a list of files that match. Don't remember

continues

continued

anything about them? That's OK, it's been awhile since you've seen the "The Least You Need to Know About DOS" at the beginning of this book. Turn back there now. I'll wait.

6. Click on **OK**.

Before you edit a configuration file, buy some cheap insurance in the form of a bootable diskette. You can then "cash it in" if the changes you make blow up in your face. Check out the FORMAT command for more info. Also, after making changes to a configuration file, you have to restart your PC for those changes to take affect. Stand back a few feet and press Ctrl + Alt + Del.

You can start EDIT with a file already open, if you want. Type the name of the file (and its directory) after the EDIT command, like this:

```
EDIT C:\AUTOEXEC.BAT
```

When you press ↵Enter after typing this command, EDIT will open with the AUTOEXEC.BAT file ready for your scapel.

EDIT: Adding a New Line

If you're working in an existing file, you can add new lines between existing lines of text if you want. If your mind comes up blank, here's what to do:

If you're creating a new file, simply type the text you want and press ↵Enter to start a new line.

1. Click at the end of the line *below* which you want to add a new blank line.

2. Press ⏎Enter.

3. Begin typing on the new line.

If your fingers get twisted while typing in your text, press ⬅Backspace and retype. You can use the Delete key to remove whatever character is silly enough to stand under the cursor (that blinking horizontal line) while you press Del. To add more blank lines, just press ⏎Enter.

EDIT: Changing Existing Text

To change or edit an existing line, exercise your editorial prerogative:

1. Click at the point where you want to begin editing.

2. **(Optional)** Change the editing mode by pressing Insert .

Pressing Insert switches you back and forth between the editing modes Insert and Overtype. In Insert mode, existing characters graciously move over to make room for new characters as you type; in Overtype mode, new characters stomp on old characters, replacing them as you type.

3. Type the correction.

EDIT: Copying or Moving Text

To copy or move text, you work with blocks. (See, it's true: you really do learn everything you need to know about life in kindergarten.) When you copy text, the original text stays put, and the copy is moved wherever you say. When you move text, the text block disappears from its current location, and with a wave of your fingers, reappears in the new location.

1. Click on the first character you want to select for moving or copying.

2. Hold down the mouse button, then drag the mouse pointer over the additional characters you want to select. The characters you select appear highlighted.

Selected text is highlighted.

3. Click on **Edit**.

4. To copy your block, click on **Copy**.

   OR

   To move your block, click on **Cut**.

5. Click on the desired location.

6. Click on **Edit**.

7. Click on **Paste**.

Why should the mouse have all the fun? Let your fingers do the walking by pressing (Ctrl) + (Insert) to copy, (⇧Shift) + (Del) to cut, and (⇧Shift) + (Insert) to paste text blocks. Yeah, I know, they could have picked easier key combinations to remember for all this stuff. But hey, it could be worse; you could be using EDLIN.

EDIT: Deleting Text

To paraphrase Lady Macbeth, "Out, #@$% character! Out, I say!"

1. Click on the first character you want to select for deletion.

2. Hold down the mouse button, then drag the mouse pointer over the additional characters you want to select. The characters you select appear highlighted.

3. Press (Del).

To delete just one character, skip this rigamorole. Just click on it and press (Del).

EDIT: Printing a File

Printing a copy of your AUTOEXEC.BAT or your CONFIG.SYS (or your little sister's diary) is easy, and gives you something to read on rainy nights when the cable's out.

1. **(Optional)** If you want to print just part of the file, select it first. Click on the first letter of the text you want, hold down the mouse button, and drag the mouse pointer to the last letter.

2. Click on **File**.

3. Click on **Print**.

Click here to print the entire file.

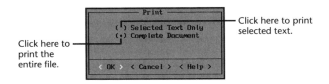

Click here to print selected text.

4. (Optional) If you only want to print part of the file, click on **Selected Text Only**.

5. Turn your printer on, and make sure it's on-line. Click on **OK**.

If nothing comes out of the dumb thing and you own a laser printer, could be the file's too short to fill a page. Force the page out by pressing the printer's Form Feed button.

EDIT: Saving a File

Saves your changes so you don't have to type them in again after you exit the Editor and discover that it doesn't do this automatically.

Saving a New File

1. Click on **File**.

2. Click on **Save**.

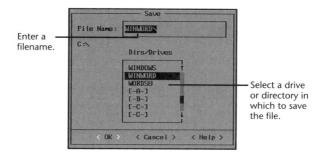

Enter a
filename.

Select a drive
or directory in
which to save
the file.

3. Type a name for the new file: *filename.ext*.

4. **(Optional)** To store the file in a different drive or
directory, double-click on that drive or directory
within the **Dirs/Drives** list.

5. Click on **OK**.

Saving a File That's Already Been Saved

1. Click on **File**.

2. Click on **Save**.

To save a file you've saved before but under a
different name or in a different directory, follow the
steps for first-time savers, but choose **SAVE AS** in
step 2.

EDIT: Exiting the DOS Editor

Before you bid EDIT a fond-farewell-and-I-hope-I-never-
see-you-again, be sure to save your work. See "EDIT:
Saving a File" in this section. To exit, stage right:

1. Click on **File**.

2. Click on **Exit**.

3. If prompted, save the file by clicking on **Yes**. If you don't want to save the file, click on **No**.

If you try to exit the program without saving, the DOS Editor will ask you if you want to save your work, or if you'd rather have it throw all your hard-earned edits into the DOS trashcan. After you get over the initial shock at its stupidity, click on **Yes** to save your file.

4. **(Optional)** If this is a new file and you haven't saved it before, complete steps 3–5 of the procedure for "EDIT: Saving a File."

More Than You'll Want to Know About Configuring Your PC

Actually, I debated about including this section. I mean, no sane person wants to know more than they might need to *about anything*, especially AUTOEXEC.BAT and CONFIG.SYS. But then I thought, one of the scariest things about using a PC is *not knowing*. Not knowing what's going on, not knowing whether something's about to blow up in your face, not knowing if the Bills are going to blow the Super Bowl again.

So you can skip this section if you want; I won't be offended. But if you stay, you'll learn the answer to important questions such as: What are all these things in my CONFIG.SYS and my AUTOEXEC.BAT? What are they doing there? And why would anyone pay good money to see Madonna in concert?

What Is the CONFIG.SYS?

The CONFIG.SYS file is a bossy file that bullies DOS into the exact configuration you need to run your programs as smoothly as possible. Some commands in the CONFIG.SYS are necessary to get certain programs to run at all, while other commands are there to improve performance (make your PC go phoom). One thing your CONFIG.SYS probably does is to load special programs called *device drivers*, which act as go-betweens for optional thingies such as a mouse, network card, tape-backup, or a CD-ROM drive. Device drivers are also used to provide access to various areas of memory (RAM). Other commands in your CONFIG.SYS probably are there to override the normal DOS settings and make your PC run your programs more efficiently.

The CONFIG.SYS is one of two configuration files, the other one being AUTOEXEC.BAT. Stay tuned for this and other exciting information on AUTOEXEC.BAT. (Be still my heart.)

A Look at Your CONFIG.SYS

To see what you've already got in your CONFIG.SYS, use our good friend the TYPE command. Follow these steps:

1. Type **C:** and press ⏎Enter.

2. Type **CD** and press ⏎Enter.

3. Type **TYPE**.

4. Press ⎵Spacebar⎵.

5. Type **CONFIG.SYS**.

6. Press ⎵Spacebar⎵.

7. Type ¦ **MORE**.

8. Press ⏎Enter.

```
H>TYPE CONFIG.SYS
DEVICE=C:\DOS\SETVER.EXE
DEVICE=C:\DOS\HIMEM.SYS
DEVICE=C:\DOS\EMM386.EXE NOEMS
BUFFERS=10,0
FILES=30
DOS=HIGH,UMB
LASTDRIVE=H
FCBS=1

STACKS=0,0

SHELL=C:\DOS\COMMAND.COM C:\DOS\ /p
DEVICEHIGH /L:1,38064 =C:\DOS\DRVSPACE.SYS /MOVE
DEVICEHIGH=h:\PWRSCSI!\ASPIFCAM.SYS
DEVICEHIGH=h:\PWRSCSI!\FDCD.SYS /D:MSCD000

H>
```

A typical CONFIG.SYS

What You're Likely to Find

Here are some commands commonly found in a
CONFIG.SYS file, and what they're doing when they're
not on coffee breaks.

> Most of these commands can be looked up in the
> special *National Enquirer* "Command Reference"
> section if you're just dying to know more about these
> guys.

Example of a Typical Command	What It Does
BREAK=ON	Gets programs to check more frequently for the secret stop-this-nonsense-now code, Ctrl+Break.
BUFFERS=20	Increases the speed of your programs by keeping the files they use in convenient areas in memory called *buffers*. Take at least 20 and call DOS in the morning.
DEVICE=C:\DOS\ HIMEM.SYS	Lets DOS access extended memory.
DEVICE=C:\DOS\ EMM386.SYS	Ah, the memories. Upper memory, that is.
DEVICE=C:\DOS\ DRVSPACE.SYS /MOVE	Loads the driver which runs your compressed drive. Do not remove under penalty of law.
DEVICE=C:\DOS\ SETVER.EXE	Allows DOS to fake its version number to fool old-fogey programs into running.

continues

Continued

Example of a Typical Command	What It Does
DEVICEHIGH=C:\ DOS\ANSI.SYS	Loads ANSI.SYS into high memory. ANSI.SYS provides access to the DOS character set, whatever that is.
DOS=HIGH	Pushes DOS out of the way and into high memory.
FILES=30	Keeps track of all those files your programs open and leave around memory.
LASTDRIVE=Z	Sets the last valid drive letter.
REM *something*	Causes DOS NOT to do *something*.
SHELL=C:\DOS\ COMMAND.COM C:\ DOS /P	Tells DOS where to find itself. Don't mess with this command without parental supervision.
STACKS=9,256	Keeps track of interrupts, which are signals that get the CPU's immediate attention. Too many interrupts and your PC will go into stack overflow toxemia, a rare but curable DOS disease.

Maximizing Your Memory Through CONFIG.SYS

If you're really interested in wrestling as much workable memory out of your PC as you can, then you've come to the right place. To make any of this work however, your

PC must be at least a 386 with a minimum of 1MB of RAM. (Hey, I can't work miracles!)

Also, since I'm in a mood to give free advice, be sure to create a bootable diskette and copy your current AUTOEXEC.BAT and CONFIG.SYS files onto it before you start messing around with them. That way, if you make a major goof and it locks up your PC, you can reboot with the diskette in drive A:. See FORMAT and COPY for help.

If you're like me, you're always looking for the easiest way out, and in this case, it's MEMMAKER. Don't expect MEMMAKER to work miracles for you either, but it tries to make the most out of the memory your system has, and it does it *automatically*. As long as you don't have multiple configurations (see "Creating a Menu System" in this part), you can use MEMMAKER without any risk to kith and kin.

If you want to attempt this on your own:

1. Type **EDIT C:\CONFIG.SYS** and press ⏎Enter.

2. On the first line, add **DEVICE=C:\DOS\HIMEM.SYS**.

3. On the next line, add **DEVICE=C:\DOS\EMM386.EXE NOEMS** or **DEVICE=C:\DOS\EMM386.EXE RAM**.

NOEMS is good to use if you have Windows; RAM is good to use if you need expanded memory for some DOS-based program (like an older version of Lotus 1-2-3 for DOS). See EMM386.EXE for more info on this elusive device driver. See the latest edition of the *National Enquirer* for details on the elusive Elvis. (I hear he was spotted recently, mumbling "Lisa-Marie and Michael? I'm all shook up.")

4. On the next line, add **DOS=HIGH,UMB**.

5. On every line which loads a device driver, replace DEVICE with **DEVICEHIGH**.

6. Click on **File** then on **Save** to save your work.

7. Click on **File** then on **Exit** to leave.

8. Reboot your computer by pressing Ctrl + Alt + Del.

9. To check your available memory, type MEM /C ¦ MORE and press ↵Enter.

More Tricks For Saving Memory

The typical CONFIG.SYS is full of fat which can be easily trimmed if you run short on memory:

FILES   Each file you specify wastes another 40 to 60 bytes of conventional memory, so use these sparingly. For most systems, 20 is a good number; if you use Windows or some other multi-tasking-keep-'em-busy-so-they-so-don't-notice-how-little-they're-being-paid environment, try 30 instead.

FCBS   Set this to 1 if you're not on a network, and reap a whopping 200 bytes of RAM.

STACKS   Windows recommends a setting of 9,128, which uses about 1KB of RAM! I use a setting of 0,0 and Windows, and I haven't seen a problem yet. If you want to run the same risk, try it and save.

BUFFERS   Each buffer you set uses 512 bytes of RAM, so again, be conservative. For most systems, 10 to 20 is a good start. If you use SMARTDrive, you can set this to a low, low 3. Use 40 if you set DOS=HIGH, because in this case, all the buffers go into high memory along with DOS—so why not splurge?

What Is the AUTOEXEC.BAT?

The AUTOEXEC.BAT is a special file that *auto*matically *exec*utes commands when you boot (start) your PC. By placing commands in the AUTOEXEC.BAT, you can make changes to the way DOS works. (Since DOS made changes to the way *you* used to work, this is only fair.) With the right commands in your AUTOEXEC.BAT, you can even make your computer start your favorite program (such as one that you use every day) automatically, while you go get some coffee or take a nap. Just turn on your PC, and whatever commands are in the AUTOEXEC.BAT, DOS just carries them out, quick as you please. It's like having your own PC butler.

The commands you place in the AUTOEXEC.BAT work at the DOS prompt too. Placing them in the AUTOEXEC.BAT simply gets your DOS butler to do them for you (saving you having to type them in manually) each time you restart your PC.

A Look Inside Your AUTOEXEC.BAT

To see what you've already got in your AUTOEXEC.BAT, use the TYPE command. Follow these steps:

1. Type **C:** and press ⏎Enter.
2. Type **CD** and press ⏎Enter.
3. Type **TYPE**.
4. Press ⎵Spacebar⎵.
5. Type **AUTOEXEC.BAT**.
6. Press ⎵Spacebar⎵.
7. Type ¦ **MORE**.
8. Press ⏎Enter.

```
H>TYPE AUTOEXEC.BAT
LOADHIGH h:\PWRSCSI†\MSCDEX.EXE /M:10 /D:MSCD000
@ECHO OFF
LH /L:0:1,45456 /S C:\DOS\SMARTDRV.EXE
LH /L:1,13904 C:\DOS\SHARE.EXE /1:500 /f:5100

C:\WINDOWS\AD_WRAP.COM
C:\DOS\MOUSE.COM

PROMPT $p$g
PATH C:\DOS;C:\WINDOWS;C:\BIN\WORD;H:\MC;H:\COLLAGE
SET TEMP=C:\WINDOWS\TEMP
SET PCPLUS=C:\PCPLUS

H>
```

A typical AUTOEXEC.BAT

What You're Likely to Find

Here are some commands commonly found in an
AUTOEXEC.BAT file, and what they're doing hanging
around there. (Remember that the commands in your
AUTOEXEC.BAT are listed *in the order in which they will
be carried out.* So if you want something to happen before
something else, you've got to place that command in
front of the others in your AUTOEXEC.BAT. Duh.)

Most of these commands can be looked up in the
"Command Reference" section if you're just dying to
know more about these guys.

Example of a Typical Command	What It Does
@ECHO OFF	Keeps your screen looking nice as the AUTOEXEC.BAT runs, by preventing extraneous stuff from displaying.
ECHO Hi there!	Causes the message **Hi there!** to display while the AUTOEXEC.BAT runs.

C:\DOS\ MOUSE.COM	Loads the driver file that makes your mouse go click.
PATH=C:\DOS;C:\ WINDOWS	Sets the directory path that DOS searches when a command or a program is not located in the current directory.
PROMPT PG	Transforms the dusty DOS prompt **C>** into a Cinderella prompt: **C:\DOS>**.
SET TEMP=C:\ WINDOWS\TEMP	Tells Windows where to keep all those darn temporary files it creates, so that later, when your PC locks up and you have to restart, you can come here and delete the silly things.
C:\DOS\ SMARTDRV.EXE	Loads SMARTDrive, which creates a RAM cache, which make PC go zoom.
C:\DOS\SHARE.EXE	Makes programs play nicely together and share files. This command is required by Windows and networks.
C:\DOS\ UNDELETE /SC	Prevents heart attacks by keeping track of deleted files on drive C (including those you delete by accident), using a method called Delete Sentry. Take one a day.

Maximizing Memory Through AUTOEXEC.BAT

The Skipper of memory management is CONFIG.SYS. AUTOEXEC.BAT is more like Gilligan: he runs around waving his hands, but in the end, only does a little. If you've set up your CONFIG.SYS file to maximize memory, then in the AUTOEXEC.BAT, you can push some TSRs (terminate-and-stay-resident programs) into upper memory and out of the way of your regularly scheduled programs. TSRs load into memory and go to "sleep" until they are awakened by a kiss, a magic keypress, or something similar.

1. Type **EDIT C:\AUTOEXEC.BAT** and press ⏎Enter to start the DOS Editor.

2. Before each line that starts a device driver or a TSR, add LH and a space: **LH** [Spacebar].

For example, to load SHARE high, change this line

   C:\DOS\SHARE.EXE

to

   LH C:\DOS\SHARE.EXE

You could go mad, mad I say! and repeat this process for other TSRs and device drivers such as DOSKEY, SMARTDRV.EXE, MOUSE.COM, VSAFE.COM or UNDELETE.COM if you want.

4. Click on **File**, then click on **Save** to save your work.

5. Click on **File**, then click on **Exit** to leave EDIT.

6. Reboot your computer by pressing Ctrl + Alt + Del simultaneously.

7. To check your available memory, type: **MEM /C ¦ MORE** and press ⏎Enter.

More Tricks to Save Memory

If you use TSRs, be sure to load them *before* you use the following commands in your AUTOEXEC.BAT:

PATH

SET

PROMPT

Why? Because I said so. OK, if you want the 25-cent explanation, here goes: each time a TSR is loaded into memory, it receives—absolutely free—a copy of the environment area (a "notepad" that DOS uses to keep track of stuff). The PATH, SET, and PROMPT commands are placed in this environment area, making it fat. So if you use these commands first, then load several TSRs, the copy of the environment area they get is larger than normal because our three musketeers (the PATH, SET, and PROMPT commands) are already present. Load the TSRs first and they get a smaller environment package that's easier to lug around.

Interrupting Your PC's Startup Procedure

After all that work trying to get your AUTOEXEC.BAT and CONFIG.SYS exactly suited to your needs, why would you ever want to skip the commands in the AUTOEXEC.BAT or CONFIG.SYS by interrupting the normal startup procedure? Good questions. Now for the answer: I don't know. I mean, I can't tell you when you might want to do that, but I can give you some good reasons. For example, suppose you're having problems with your PC. Big-time puzzling problems. You might want to avoid the CONFIG.SYS if you'd just made changes to it, and those changes caused your PC to do the mambo. Or maybe your AUTOEXEC.BAT always starts Windows, and today, you don't want it to.

Bypassing Your Configuration Files

1. Wait until you see the words, **Starting MS-DOS**.

2. Then press F5.

Bypassing Some Commands, But Not Others

1. Wait until you see the words, **Starting MS-DOS**.

2. Press F8.

3. You'll be prompted to bypass or execute each command. Press Y to execute a command, or N to skip it.

4. Next, you'll be prompted to run the AUTOEXEC.BAT. Press Y to run it, or N to skip it.

5. If you run the AUTOEXEC.BAT, press Y or N again to select the commands you want to execute.

6. **(Optional)** If at some point you want simply to execute the remaining commands, press Esc. To bypass the remaining commands instead of running them, press F5.

Creating a Menu System

DOS 6.x allows you to customize your CONFIG.SYS making it possible for you to start your computer in a number of ways, depending on what you feel like doing today. For example, you have two programs with very different needs (such as Lotus 1-2-3 for DOS, which uses expanded memory, and Windows, which does not). You can set up a menu which configures you system one way when you select Lotus, and another when you select Windows. In addition, you can add commands to your AUTOEXEC.BAT to run programs based on the menu selection you choose from the CONFIG.SYS.

These multiple configurations, by the way, actually go into a single CONFIG.SYS, so all you really have to do is add some more commands to your CONFIG.SYS to divide it into two sections. More on that coming up.

How to Select an Option From a Startup Menu

To give you a way to choose between your CONFIG.SYS twins, you need to add a menu to your CONFIG.SYS. You'll probably want to write these commands down, then jump back to the section, "Hacking Away at Your Files With the DOS Editor" to get instructions on editing your CONFIG.SYS. Or you can write down these commands, buy a six-pack of whatever, and bribe a friend to make the changes for you. First, let's take a look at what our finished menu's going to look like.

```
MS DOS 6.22 Startup Menu


     1. Lotus 1-2-3 for DOS
     2. Windows Only


  Enter a choice:      Time remaining: 18
```

When the PC starts up, our sample menu is displayed. To choose an option:

1. Type the number of your choice.

2. Press (↵Enter).

The commands in the appropriate part of your CONFIG.SYS are then carried out. Simple as that.

Defining Your Menu

To set up a menu (if you want to sneak a peek at a completed CONFIG.SYS, jump ahead to the next figure):

1. Type **EDIT C:\CONFIG.SYS** and press (↵Enter).

2. At the beginning of the file, type **[MENU]** and press (↵Enter).

This command really doesn't do much but help you create a separate section in your CONFIG.SYS for the commands which create the menu. Think of this as putting up a fence. In step 3, we'll add the cattle (the actual commands that will make the menu work).

3. Type **MENUITEM=**.

4. Type a label for your selection, followed by a comma and a description (like this: *LABEL, description*). Press ⊷Enter.

For example, type:

```
MENUITEM=LOTUS, Lotus 1-2-3 for DOS
```

to add the menu option, "Lotus 1-2-3 for DOS" to the menu. The label "LOTUS" is used later in the CONFIG.SYS to tell DOS what commands to execute when this menu option is chosen.

5. Repeat step 4 to add additional menu items. (Each menu item *must* have a unique *label*.)

For example, type

```
MENUITEM=WIN, Windows Programs
```

to create a second menu option for Windows.

6. (**Optional**) To designate one of the menu options as the default, type **MENUDEFAULT=** followed by the label of the menu option, a comma, and the

number of seconds you want DOS to wait for the
user to select a different option. Press ↵Enter.

Try This!

For example, to make the Windows option the default
after waiting 20 seconds, type:

MENUDEFAULT=WIN,20

In this example, WIN is the label associated with the
MENUITEM "Windows Programs".

7. Press ↵Enter to insert a blank line.

8. Type one of the labels used earlier in the
   MENUITEM command, surrounded by square
   brackets (like this: **[*label*]**). Press ↵Enter

9. Type the commands you want executed when this
   menu option is selected.

10. Press ↵Enter to insert a blank line between sec-
    tions.

11. Repeat steps 8 through 10 to add additional
    sections, one for each MENUITEM used earlier.

Try This!

For example, suppose you were creating a menu
system to let you choose between configuring your
PC for Lotus 1-2-3 for DOS and Windows. You might
add the following commands:

```
[LOTUS]
DEVICE=C:\DOS\HIMEM.SYS
DEVICE=C:\DOS\EMM386.EXE RAM 2048
DOS=HIGH,UMB
FILES=20
```

continues

continued

```
BUFFERS=30,0
DEVICEHIGH=C:\DOS\DRVSPACE.SYS /MOVE

[WIN]
DEVICE=C:\DOS\HIMEM.SYS
DEVICE=C:\DOS\EMM386.EXE NOEMS
DOS=HIGH,UMB
FILES=40
BUFFERS=10,0
DEVICEHIGH=C:\DOS\DRVSPACE.SYS /MOVE
```

12. Click on **File** and **Save** to save your changes.

13. Click on **File** and **Exit** to exit EDIT.

These commands
create a menu.

```
 File  Edit  Search  Options                                    Help
                        ═══════ CONFIG.SYS ═══════
[MENU]
MENUITEM=LOTUS, Lotus 1-2-3 for DOS
MENUITEM=WIN, Windows Programs
MENUDEFAULT=WIN,20

[LOTUS]
DEVICE=C:\DOS\HIMEM.SYS
DEVICE=C:\EMM386.EXE RAM 2048
DOS=HIGH,UMB
FILES=20
BUFFERS=30,0
DEVICEHIGH=C:\DOS\DRVSPACE.SYS /MOVE

[WIN]
DEVICE=C:\DOS\HIMEM.SYS
DEVICE=C:\DOS\EMM386.EXE NOEMS
DOS=HIGH,UMB
FILES=40
BUFFERS=10,0
DEVICEHIGH=C:\DOS\DRVSPACE.SYS /MOVE

 MS-DOS Editor  <F1=Help> Press ALT to activate menus          N 00001:001
```

These two sections provide the CONFIG.SYS
commands to be carried out, depending on
which menu selection is chosen at startup.

You can do other neat things with your menu, such as
creating a [COMMON] area to hold commands which
are the same for both choices (notice that we have a lot

of repetition here). See the INCLUDE command for more help in that area. Heck, you can even change the colors on your menu if you want; see the MENUCOLOR command.

You can also create a menu system with submenus (see—what else?—the SUBMENU command). For example, you could have a menu choice called Games, and a submenu listing various games you play. That way, each game could be set up with its own private configuration, since each game is listed as a different selection on the menu.

Adding Menu Stuff to Your AUTOEXEC.BAT

Why should your CONFIG.SYS have all the fun? You can have DOS execute different commands in your AUTOEXEC.BAT on the basis of the *menu item chosen from the CONFIG.SYS.*

1. Type **C:\AUTOEXEC.BAT** and press ⏎Enter.

2. Type **GOTO %CONFIG%** and press ⏎Enter.

You can place the GOTO command below any commands you want to execute regardless of which menu item is chosen. For example, you'll probably always want to load the mouse driver, so place the GOTO command after the command, C:\DOS\MOUSE.COM in your AUTOEXEC.BAT.

3. Type a colon followed by a label used in one of MENUITEM commands in the CONFIG.SYS (like this: **:LABEL**). Press ⏎Enter.

Try This!

For example, type

:LOTUS

to match with the command MENUITEM=LOTUS,
Lotus 1-2-3 for DOS used earlier in the CONFIG.SYS.

4. Type the commands you want executed when this
   option is chosen from the menu, each on a
   separate line.

5. Type **GOTO END** and press [↵Enter].

6. Press [↵Enter] to create a blank line between sections.

7. Repeat steps 3 through 6 for each MENUITEM
   command used in the CONFIG.SYS.

8. Type **:END**.

9. Click on **File** and **Save** to save your changes.

10. Click on **File** and **Exit** to exit EDIT.

These commands are always executed.

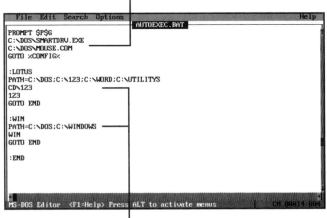

```
   File  Edit  Search  Options                              Help
                            █ AUTOEXEC.BAT █
PROMPT $P$G
C:\DOS\SMARTDRV.EXE
C:\DOS\MOUSE.COM
GOTO %CONFIG%

:LOTUS
PATH=C:\DOS;C:\123;C:\WORD;C:\UTILITYS
CD\123
123
GOTO END

:WIN
PATH=C:\DOS;C:\WINDOWS
WIN
GOTO END

:END



MS-DOS Editor  <F1=Help> Press ALT to activate menus        CH 00014:004
```

Only one of these sets of commands is carried out,
depending on which menu option is selected at startup.

For example, consider this AUTOEXEC.BAT. The PROMPT and the SMARTDRV commands are already familiar. They're executed regardless of which menu option is chosen from the startup menu. The GOTO command tells DOS to go get the selection made when the CONFIG.SYS was run.

Now for the fun part. The :LOTUS command creates a section in the AUTOEXEC.BAT similar to the [LOTUS] command in the CONFIG.SYS. Underneath it are the commands that are carried out when the user chooses choice number 1 from the startup menu. The GOTO END command tells it to then go to the :END marker at the end of the file, cheerfully skipping over the :WIN section of commands.

If the user chooses number 2 (Windows), then DOS jumps over the :LOTUS section and performs only the commands in the :WIN section. It then gets to the :END marker, which means that the startup procedure is finito.

Common DOS Error Messages

There are few things more cryptic than DOS error messages (except maybe a tax form, the meaning behind a Calvin Klein commercial, or my handwriting). Even veteran users can't always tell what DOS means when it issues an error—but don't worry—in this section, you'll find the cures for what ails you. Here you'll find a listing of the most common DOS error messages, complete with a list of what happened and what you should do now.

Abort, Retry, Ignore, Fail?

See "General failure reading (or writing) drive x. Abort, Retry, Fail?"

Access Denied

You tried to delete or edit a file that's protected. Don't do that! You should probably not delete or edit this file, because files are usually protected for a reason. If you feel that you need to delete or edit this file, ask a PC guru for advice.

If you're the super-gung-ho-go-for-it type, you can use the ATTRIB command to unprotect the file, then delete it. But don't tell anyone I told you to do that.

All files in directory will be deleted! Are you sure (Y/N)?

Silly you! You're trying to delete a directory, which is non-removable under penalty of law. OK, just kidding. If you want to say "Adios, directory," press Y. If you've had a change of heart and you just can't say goodbye, press N.

ANSI.SYS must be installed to perform requested function

The program you are trying to run requires ANSI.SYS, a device driver that provides access to the DOS extended character set, whatever that is. You're gonna hate this one, 'cause it means editing your CONFIG.SYS file. Add this command:

```
DEVICE=C:\DOS\ANSI.SYS
```

Then reboot your computer by pressing ⌜Ctrl⌟ + ⌜Alt⌟ + ⌜Del⌟ and try again.

Bad command or file name

Your fingers got fouled up and you mistyped the command, OR: the command is a figment of your overworked imagination, OR: it's an external DOS command and you're not in the DOS directory, so DOS can't find it. If it's a DOS command you're trying to enter, try typing it again, and don't add extra spaces where they're not needed (add one after the command, and between switches). If it doesn't work, change to the DOS directory (**CD\DOS**).

If you're trying to start a program, change to the directory where the program lives (**CD\program**). If it still doesn't work, make sure you have the right name for the program (**DIR *.EXE**).

Bad or missing Command Interpreter

You've just exited a program that you started from a diskette, OR: your PC has temporarily lost its "brain." (The COMMAND.COM file that is normally in the root directory of your C drive has been deleted accidentally, or—while copying all the files from a diskette—you've copied an older version of the COMMAND.COM file onto your drive.)

To fix this problem, if you were running a program from a diskette and removed it, then try sneaking the thing back into its drive and pressing R for Retry. If that doesn't work, reboot the computer with Ctrl + Alt + Del and it should be OK.

If you're PC doesn't have a brain, then click your heels three times, and with your emergency diskette in drive A, reboot the computer (press Ctrl + Alt + Del).

Then type this command: `COPY A:COMMAND.COM C:`.

An *emergency diskette* is a bootable disk which contains three files: COMMAND.COM, IO.SYS, and MSDOS.SYS (the last two are hiding, which means you can't see them but they're there). A good emergency diskette should also contain recent copies of your AUTOEXEC.BAT and CONFIG.SYS, for times like this where your PC takes an unplanned vacation.

Bad sectors

After you've formatted a diskette, a number of bad sectors may be displayed. The diskette may be damaged, or you may have formatted the diskette to the wrong density.

Verify that you formatted the diskette to the proper density, or try formatting it again. If the diskette appears damaged, don't use it for anything but a frisbee.

Cannot execute x

See "Error in EXE file."

Cannot make directory entry

Your disk's root directory is more full than a fat man at Thanksgiving. There's just no more room for the file or the directory you're trying to make. Delete some files or directories from the root directory and try again.

Current drive is no longer valid>

You jumped the gun and removed a diskette before a
function was complete, or you were trying to use a
diskette drive that didn't have a diskette in it. So, Fast
Fingers, put that diskette back in the diskette drive. If
you want to make drive A the current drive, type **A:** at
the prompt. If you want to return to drive C, type **C:** at
the prompt and press ⏎Enter.

Data error reading drive x Abort, Retry, Fail?

A file was damaged and your PC is having a tough time
making heads or tails of it. Press R for Retry. If that
doesn't work and the message returns, press A for
Abort, then try to locate another copy of the file (say, on
a backup—you know, that thing you said you'd do as
soon as you found the time), and use it instead. If you
have any disk utilities (such as Norton Utilities), you
might be able to repair the damaged diskette.

Directory already exists

You're trying to create a directory, but you're not feeling
terribly original, so you've entered the same name of a
directory that already exists. Choose a different name
and try again.

Disk boot failure

DOS is having a hard time getting started this morning.
Restart your computer with Ctrl + Alt + Del and try
again.

If the problem persists, circle the wagons, turn off the
computer's power, wait 30 seconds, and try again. Still
no luck? Boot from a floppy disk and use SYS to
retransfer the DOS system files onto your hard disk. If
that fails, your PC should make an interesting doorstop.

Divide overflow

The program you were just running tried to divide
something by zero, causing your PC to scratch its head

and finally give up. First off, grin, because you've just seen absolute proof of how stupid computers are. If you feel like it, restart your program and try to duplicate the error. Call the technical support for the program, and tell them to send out the goof squad or a refund pronto.

Drive types or diskette types not compatible
Copy process ended
Copy another diskette (Y/N)?

You're trying to use DISKCOPY with disks that aren't the same. Good try, but no cigar. DISKCOPY only works with the same size and the same density diskettes. Otherwise, you must use COPY or XCOPY.

Duplicate file name or file not found

You used the REN command to rename a file, but the new filename already exists. Sorry, there are already too many Smiths. Try the command with another name, as in:

```
REN OLDFILE.DOC NEWFILE.DOC
```

Error in EXE file

The program file you are trying to run has somehow been damaged or tampered with, so it can't come out to play. Recopy it from the original diskette that it came on.

Error in loading operating system

DOS is having trouble getting started, and it could use some real strong coffee right about now (probably so could you). Reboot (press Ctrl + Alt + Del) and try again.

If DOS just won't wake up, then boot from your emergency diskette, and recopy the system files to your hard disk with the command **SYS C:**. If that fails, contact a computer dealer and see if he wants a new nightstand.

Error reading drive x

See "General failure reading drive x."

Execute failure

Take two aspirin then try the remedies listed under
"Error in EXE file." If you don't have any success,
increase the number on the FILES= line in your
CONFIG.SYS file.

Fail on INT 24

Most likely, your finger got stuck on the F key when you
were repeatedly offered the choices of "Abort, Retry,
Fail." After correcting the problem that caused the
"Abort, Retry, Fail" message in the first place, try what
you were doing again.

File allocation table bad, drive x Abort, Retry, Fail?

The diskette you're trying to use is on big-time drugs.
Try choosing ⒭ for Retry several times. If it doesn't
work, choose Ⓐ for Abort. Copy all the data you can
salvage off the diskette, then throw it into the round file.

If you got this message while trying to use the hard
drive, you may be in big trouble. Cross your fingers and
think back to the last time you did a backup (and hope
it's sometime recently). Salvage what you can, then
reformat the disk (FORMAT). This is a drastic step, so
you may want to call in the cavalry and try a disk
recovery program like Norton Utilities first.

File cannot be copied onto itself

You just tried the COPY command, but you left out
some important stuff, such as a new directory or drive
for the file or a new name. First of all, don't do that. If
you type something shorthand like COPY JENNY.DOC,
DOS doesn't know what to do. Copy JENNY.DOC
where? Be sure to specify complete paths when copying
a file, as in COPY JENNY.DOC A: or COPY JENNY.DOC
NEWJENNY.DOC.

File creation error

You're sitting in your program, trying to save a new file, when all of a sudden, zap! Well, first make sure the filename you're trying to use is unique. Next, make sure that the root directory that you're trying to save the file in isn't full. If it is, get rid of something!

Disks vary as to how many files their root directories can hold. For a floppy, it's somewhere just over 100; for a hard disk, it's around 500.

File is READ-ONLY

You're trying to access a read-only file. Well, you shouldn't do that. Because files are set to read-only for a reason, you should try something else. Like ping-pong. If you're desperate and you promise not to tell where you got this info, use ATTRIB to change the file's attributes and try again.

File not found

You mistyped the filename or the path to the file while trying to enter a DOS command, OR: the file you referred to in the command does not exist except in your imagination.

First, get rid of that frown; it's probably just that darn backslash again. Verify the path you are using, and make sure that you type a backslash (\) to separate the parts of a path, as in C:\PROJECTS\DRU\CHAP01.DOC. You can also try the command again, but with a different (truly there) kind of file.

This message also occurs, harmlessly, if you type **DEL** *.* in a directory that's already empty. So don't do dat.

General failure (reading or writing) drive x

There's a smorgasbord of reasons for this one; we'll handle them one at a time. First off, in your big rush to do something with DOS, you may have forgotten to format your diskette. I know DOS is really exciting, but slow down. Press ⒡ for Fail, then format the diskette to its proper density by typing something like FORMAT A: / V.

OR: The diskette in the drive you referred to was damaged, and could not be read or written to. Replace with another diskette and press ⒭ for Retry, or press ⒡ for Fail, and reformat this diskette.

OR: You used the wrong type of diskette, such as a high-density diskette in a double-density drive. First off, don't do that. If you have to, then reformat the high-density diskette as double-density, or use a diskette of the proper type.

OR: The diskette in the drive you referred to may not be placed in the drive properly, or you left the drive door open. Just goes to show you that when you leave the door open, you just don't know who may come in. Remove the diskette from its drive, and verify that it is placed properly in the drive. If necessary, tap the diskette on the side to make sure the diskette material has not shifted in the sleeve. And for gosh sakes, close the door—there's a draft!

OR: There's a possibility that the drive you referred to is having problems. If you were trying to use the hard disk, this could be the first indicator of some major problems. Better get a PC guru help you test your hard disk.

OR: If you were trying to start a program, this could indicate a problem with the program files. If you get this error with a variety of programs, the problem is more likely your hard disk. Again, have a PC guru help you test your hard disk. They may recommend re-installing the program.

Incorrect DOS version

The command you're trying to run doesn't work with
the version of DOS your PC's using. If the command is a
DOS command, you've somehow gotten files from
different versions of DOS onto your system, which is a
bad idea, since as you've just found out, that doesn't
work. You may have to reinstall DOS to get it straight-
ened out.

If the command you just tried to use is an application
program, it may so old that it requires an earlier version
of DOS than the one you have. Try mouth-to-mouth
resusitation, then try to fool it with the SETVER command.

Insufficient disk space

There's no room at the inn. You tried to copy a file onto
a diskette, and there was not enough room. Delete some
files from the diskette to make room for the files you
want, or reuse the COPY command with another
diskette.

Insufficient memory

Your PC's awfully tired about now. If you were trying to
start a program, and you got this message, you have too
many things in memory (RAM), and you need to unload
some of them. Exit as many programs as possible, then
retry the command. If necessary, reboot the computer by
pressing Ctrl + Alt + Del.

Rebooting causes a computer's memory to clear. If you
still have a problem, try eliminating some of the
memory-resident programs from your AUTOEXEC.BAT,
and some of the infrequently needed drivers from your
CONFIG.SYS. Then reboot and try again. See the section,
"More Than You'll Want to Know About Configuring
Your PC."

Internal stack overflow. System halted

Your PC's been interrupted by too many keypresses or
too many mouse clicks, or too many requests from your

program. Anyway, it got so busy, it just blew its stack. So first, slow down, Mario. If this error occurs once, reboot and ignore it. If it occurs frequently, increase the available stacks with the STACKS= command in your CONFIG.SYS file. See "STACKS" in the Command Reference section.

Invalid characters in volume label

You were trying desperately to come up with an understandable diskette label using only eleven miserly characters, and you used characters that DOS considers "inappropriate." Tsk. Retype the label and get rid of the offensive little guy. Characters that are invalid include:

```
* ? / \ | . , ; : + = [ ]
```

Invalid COMMAND.COM

Dive! Dive! Your COMMAND.COM file's been breached, and water's coming in everywhere. Reboot your computer using a bootable floppy diskette (your emergency diskette that you keep for times like this). Then copy COMMAND.COM from that diskette onto the root directory of drive C:.

Invalid date

You typed a date incorrectly, or you typed a date which only exists in your vivid imagination. Try it again using a valid format—for example, 10-16-94, 10/16/94, or for those you love to be different, 10.16.94.

Invalid directory

You are trying to change to a directory that doesn't exist except in fairy tales, you're misspelling the name, or you forgot to place a backslash between the parts of the directory path (as in C:\WORD\DOCS). Check your typing and try again. To get a list of the directories to choose from, type this command:

```
DIR C:\*. /S /P
```

Invalid drive in search path

One of the entries in your PATH statement is nonexistent. You're referring to a disk drive that doesn't exist, or
has been hidden temporarily by a SUBST or JOIN
command. Well, you've been caught. Edit the PATH
command in your AUTOEXEC.BAT to correct the error.

Invalid drive specification

You referred to a drive that doesn't exist, or you referred
to a network drive before you logged onto the network.
Check your typing and try again. (If it's a network drive,
log on, then try again.)

Invalid filename or file not found

You tried to use wildcard characters with the TYPE
command, as in TYPE *.BAT (sorry, no can do), OR: You
tried to rename a file with an invalid filename. Try
renaming the file to something else (gee, I would never
have thought of that).

Invalid media or Track 0
Bad _ disk unusable
Format Terminated
Format another (Y/N)?

You're trying to format a disk to the wrong density, or
the diskette was badly damaged. Use a different diskette,
or specify a different capacity with the /F switch in your
FORMAT command. If that doesn't work, see if you can
find three more damaged diskettes and make a coaster
set.

Invalid parameter or Invalid switch

There's a list of reasons for this one, so we'll take them
one at a time. First, you might have used a parameter or
switch that's invalid for this command. Don't do that.
Look up the command in the command reference
section, and follow the example carefully.

OR: You entered a space between the forward slash and
the character when entering a switch, as in DIR / W.
Such a character! If you want to enter a switch for a
command, there's no need for a space between the
forward slash (/) and the character. Type the command
like this: **DIR** **/W**. You'll have better luck. Believe me.

OR: You used a backward slash (\) when specifying a
switch. Those darn slashes! Use a forward slash for
switches, as in **DIR** **/W** and not its evil sibling DIR \W. To
keep them straight, here's a tip from my "Hunt-and-Peck
Guide to Typing DOS Commands": the backslash is
usually located West of Honolulu, and North of the Enter
key, on the same key as another hard to find character,
the pipe (|).)

OR: You used a forward slash (/) when specifying a
filename path. How silly of you to use logic at a time like
this. Use a backward slash (\) when specifying the path
to a file, as in **C:\WORD\NEW.DOC**.

Invalid path

You made up the directory path to a file, or you
mistyped a directory name. Verify the correct path and
retype the command.

Invalid path, not directory, or directory not empty

You're trying to remove a current directory that isn't
empty or doesn't exist. Delete the files first, then delete
the directory. Or, if you're real smart (and real lazy) use
the DELTREE command instead, because it deletes all the
files for you, then removes the directory.

OR: You're trying to delete a file using the RD command.
Wrongo. Go back two spaces and use the DEL command
instead.

Invalid switch

You either got inventive and added a switch to a command that doesn't use any, or you made up a new one.
In either case, check out the valid switches in the
command reference section, and try, try, again.

Memory allocation error
Cannot load MS-DOS, system halted

A program you've been running has messed up DOS's memory so bad, it's remembering as poorly as Ronald Reagan at the Iran-Contra hearings. Reboot your system and try again. If the problem insists on staying around, boot from a floppy disk and use SYS to copy the system files to your hard disk.

No Path

You've typed PATH to see what your path is set to, but were greeted by this sad statement instead. It means that you don't have a path set up yet. Type **PATH=** and then the drives and directories you want to include in the path.

If you want to forget this ever happened, put the PATH= line in your AUTOEXEC.BAT file so you don't have to type it every time you restart your PC.

Non-System disk or disk error
Replace and press any key when ready

You left a diskette in drive A while you booted the computer. Oops! Remove the diskette and press ⌈Ctrl⌉ + ⌈Alt⌉ + ⌈Del⌉ at the same time.

Do *not* press "any key to continue," as the screen suggests, because you run the risk of transmitting a virus to your system if the diskette is infected. (See, DOS doesn't know everything!)

OR: There's no diskette, and you were simply trying to boot from the hard disk. Uh-oh. This could been big-time trouble, so call the cavalry to help.

Not ready reading drive x
Abort, Retry, Fail?

You typed a command that referred to a diskette drive, and there's nothing in that drive. Oops! Place a diskette in the drive, then press ⬚R⬚ for Retry. If you want to give up and go home because you're obviously overworked, press ⬚A⬚ for Abort.

OR: You didn't close the diskette drive door. You're letting in flies, so close the door and press ⬚R⬚ for Retry.

Overwrite xxxxxxxx.xxx (yes/no/all)?

You had the nerve to try moving or copying files on top of existing versions of those same files. Press ⬚Y⬚ to overwrite each file, or press ⬚A⬚ to overwrite them all, or ⬚N⬚ to skip it.

Packed file is corrupt

You tried running a program and got this message. The problem is long and involved, and basically who cares anyway, since you need to leave early today and you've still got too much to do? Type **LOADFIX,** a space, and then the program name. For example, type **LOADFIX WORDSTAR** and press ⬚⏎Enter⬚.

Parameter format not correct

You aren't using the correct parameters for the command you're typing. Why? I don't know. Review the parameters for that command and try again.

Path not found

You got fancy and included a directory path within a command, and the only trouble is that *it doesn't exist.* Retype the command with the correct directory path, or just go on home, 'cause you must be awfully tired.

Press any key to continue...

This is not an error message. (Isn't that a kick?) DOS is pausing while it waits for you to do something, such as switch diskettes in a drive, or read the display. When you are ready to continue, you can press any key on the keyboard, such as the Enter key. Do not look for a key called "Any." Although it sounds as if there should be a specific key you should press, you can actually press any key you want.

Printer out of paper error writing device PRN Abort, Retry, Ignore, Fail?

Your printer is hungry and it's past dinnertime. Load some paper, and press ⒭ for Retry.

Program too big to fit in memory

DOS thinks it doesn't have enough room in RAM for your big-fat-got-so-many-features-you'll-be-lucky-to-use-half-of-them program. Reboot and try again. If the problem won't go away, you may not have enough memory to run the big-fat-you-know-the-rest; check the program's requirements.

Read fault error reading drive x Abort, Retry, Fail?

Your PC can't read, or it needs glasses. Press ⒭ for Retry to try again.

If that doesn't work, try removing and reinserting the disk. If that doesn't work, your disk may be usable only as a frisbee.

Required parameter missing

You left out some important part of the command. Geez, picky, picky. Review the parameters for the command, and then try it again.

Sector not found
Abort, Retry, Fail?

Your file's "off the map." In other words, there may be physical damage to the diskette (or to the diskette drive) that's preventing DOS from locating your file. Try ⒭ for Retry a few times; if that doesn't work, choose Ⓐ and quit trying. For an interesting experiment, try a different diskette to determine whether the problem is your drive or your diskette.

If you get this error while trying to access your hard drive, contact your dealer and ask him where he got this piece of junk. The problem could be the hard disk, the hard disk controller, or something on the motherboard. Whatever, as long as *he* pays for repairs.

Seek error
Abort, Retry, Fail?

Your file's playing hide-and-*seek* with DOS, and DOS isn't very good at it. Reinsert the diskette, and then press ⒭ for Retry. If the problem persists with different diskettes, you may have a tracking problem with your drive; contact your dealer with your best ranting and raving voice.

Sharing violation
Abort, Retry, Fail?

You're running a program that's selfish. So it'll learn to share and play nicely with others, exit to the DOS prompt if you're not already there, type SHARE, and then try again.

Source diskette bad or incompatible

When using the DISKCOPY command, you tried to use your two diskette drives, but they're not the same type. Don't do that. If the two diskette drives are different types (densities), you'll have to use one drive to do your disk copying, as in **DISKCOPY B: B:**.

Specified drive does not exist or is non-removable

When using the DISKCOPY command, you specified a hard disk drive, or a nonexistent drive. First, make sure you specify valid drive letters that come from this universe. Then use only diskette drive letters with the DISKCOPY command, as in **DISKCOPY A: A:**.

Syntax error

You used the wrong format when typing a command. Why? Probably 'cause you didn't want to look it up, even though now you're stuck with looking up the error message. Well, just go look up the command, and this time type it in correctly.

TARGET diskette bad or incompatible Copy process ended

You're minding your own business, trying to duplicate a diskette with DISKCOPY, and you now you discover (courtesy of this DOS error message) that the target diskette is a different type than the source diskette. Unfortunately, there's no way around this; the two diskettes must be the same. Find an appropriate diskette to be your target disk, and try again.

Track 0 bad diskette unusable

There are bad sectors near the beginning of the diskette that's preventing it from being formatted. If that's the case, throw the diskette away (or return it to the manufacturer for a heart-felt apology).

OR: You may be trying to format a diskette to a wrong density. Uh-oh. Try using the /F switch with the FORMAT command to specify a density that's right.

Too many parameters

Your busy fingers were flying so fast, you typed more than you needed to, such as more than one command on a line. Slow down, Mario, and try again—typing only one command at a time, and pressing ⏎Enter between each one.

Unable to write BOOT

You're trying to format a bootable diskette, but the thing is so badly damaged (was *that* the crunch you heard when you backed up your chair a moment ago?) that it can't be done. Write the diskette off on your taxes, and try another one.

Unrecognized command in CONFIG.SYS
Error in CONFIG.SYS line x

Well, no one can blame you for trying. You just edited your CONFIG.SYS, and you typed a boo-boo. Edit CONFIG.SYS and correct the typo. Then reboot your system.

WARNING ALL DATA ON NON-REMOV-ABLE DISK
DRIVE X: WILL BE LOST!
Proceed with Format (Y/N)?

Well now, what *have* you been up to? Most likely, you were using the FORMAT command, and you accidentally used the letter of the hard disk drive. OR: You're nutso and you want to format your hard disk *and lose all the data on it.* Press Y to format your hard disk (you crazy critter), or N to get out of there fast before something happens.

Write failure, diskette unusable

There's a problem with the diskette you're using to create a bootable diskette. Darn. Discard the diskette, or return it to the manufacturer for a refund.

Write fault error writing device PRN

You've forgotten to turn your printer on. Wake up, and turn it on now.

Write fault error writing drive x
Abort, Retry, Fail?

DOS can't write something and it really, really wants to.
If the trouble is a diskette, it's probably inserted wrong;
remove the disk and reinsert it, and then press ⒭ for
Retry.

If the problem persists, discard the diskette or return it to
the manufacturer for a refund, using your best don't-
mess-with-me-I've-been-fooling-with-my-darn-PC-all-
day-and-I'm-late-with-that-report-again voice.

Write protect error writing drive x
Abort, Retry, Fail?

The diskette you're trying to copy something to is write-
protected. Probably for good reason, so get another
diskette. If you really want to do this, remove the write-
protect tab (if it's a 5 1/4-inch diskette) or move the
write-protect switch to cover the "hole" (if it's a 3 1/2-
inch diskette), and then press ⒭ for Retry. If you've
regained your sanity and decided that you don't want to
copy the file, press ⒜ for Abort.

Index